CURE YOUR MONEY ILLS

Improve Your Self-Esteem Through Personal Budgeting

MICHAEL R. SLAVIT, Ph.D.

R & E Publishers ❖ Saratoga, California

Copyright © 1992 by Michael R. Slavit

All rights reserved.

This book is sold with the understanding that the subject matter covered herein is of a general nature and does not constitute legal, accounting or other professional advice for any specific individual or situation. Anyone planning to take action in any of the areas that this book describes should, of course, seek professional advice from accountants, lawyers, tax, and other advisers, as would be prudent and advisable under their given circumstances.

R & E Publishers
P.O. Box 2008, Saratoga, CA 95070
Tel: (408) 866-6303   Fax: (408) 866-0825

Book Design by Diane Parker

Library of Congress Card Catalog Number: 91-50987

ISBN 0-88247-915-6

Acknowledgment

The author wishes to express his deepest appreciation
to his parents, Leonard and Irma Slavit, for over
forty years of unfailing love and support.

ABOUT THE AUTHOR

Dr. Michael Slavit received his Bachelors Degree in Psychology from Brown University in 1970. He received his Masters Degree in Counselor Education from the University of Rhode Island in 1975, and his Ph.D. in Counseling Psychology from the University of Texas at Austin in 1983. Dr. Slavit has been employed in university counseling centers for the past 12 years. He is licensed as a psychologist in two states, and is currently Director of Counseling at Southern College of Technology in Marietta, Georgia.

Though primarily a psychotherapist and administrator, he has had a continuing interest in financial matters for a number of years. He decided that his most useful contribution to this field would be one focusing on his understanding of the psychological aspects of personal finances. He developed the BUDGET ACCOUNT SYSTEM in 1986, and has presented it to adult continuing education students, faculty and staff at the University of Georgia and at Southern College of Technology, and to professionals at regional conferences. He has taught the system to a large number of individual clients. It has been very well received by all. The BUDGET ACCOUNT SYSTEM was created to help people achieve a sense of comfort and personal mastery while managing their finances.

In addition to personal budgeting, Dr. Slavit's professional areas of expertise include assertiveness, stress management, hypnosis, romantic relationships, and dealing with the blues.

Contents

Appendices

1 Who Can Benefit from the Budget Account System?

You can almost certainly benefit from the BUDGET ACCOUNT SYSTEM. The system was designed to help you avoid the uncomfortable, sometimes even psychologically destructive, emotions which can accompany disorganized finances.

To be sure that you can benefit, please read the following four scenarios, and then ask yourself whether you have ever had a similar experience:

Scenario # 1

You receive some money, such as an income tax refund. You say "Great! I'm going to use that money for _____" (Fill in the blank. It could be toy, vacation, investment, etcetera). You then put the money into your regular checking or savings account. Before too long, that money seems to have been "absorbed into your regular cash flow." By the time you are ready to make the expenditure that you had planned, you can no longer identify that money, or even be sure it's there. So you cannot make the expenditure with the comfortable feeling of knowing where the money came from.

(Have you ever experienced anything like that? ___yes ___no)

Scenario # 2

You go on vacation, feeling that you work hard and deserve to spend money for a pleasant and rewarding vacation. However, you do not have any money set aside to pay for the vacation. Still, you are convinced you deserve it, and you decide to charge the expenses to a credit card. You make the expenditures, and may have a pretty good time. But, you have a persistent feeling of wanting to keep expenses down. And you have a nagging worry about paying the debt.

(Have you ever experienced anything like that? ___yes ___no)

Scenario # 3

Your car seems to be having some kind of trouble. You feel "put upon" and upset. You may even delay having a mechanic look at your car. When you do have the car looked at, you're nervous while awaiting the mechanic's diagnosis. If the repair turns out to be an expensive one, you're even more upset. You wonder: "Where is the money going to come from?"

(Have you ever experienced anything like that? ___yes ___no)

Scenario # 4

You have the chance to buy something you've been wanting (for example, recreational equipment, electronics device, art object, toy, etcetera). You look in your check book, and it looks as though you have the money available. You can't think of any expenses coming up which might prevent you from making the purchase. But, you just can't free yourself from one of the following thoughts:

a) My car hasn't needed repair for awhile. Maybe "it's due." Maybe I should put the money aside for it.

b) Hey, when is my next automobile insurance premium due? I wonder if I should put the money aside for it.

c) Aren't my membership dues coming up? I wonder if I should put the money aside for them?

In short, although you may make the purchase, you cannot do so without doubts. You just can't enjoy spending the money.

(Have you ever experienced anything like that? ___yes ___no)

If you answered "no" to *all* the above scenarios, then you have one of the following:

A. Enough wealth not to worry about expenses;

B. A very systematic, organized approach to your finances;

C. A very relaxed, "devil-may-care" attitude about money; or

D. Resistance to admitting some of your uncomfortable experiences with money matters.

If you answered "yes" to one or more of the above 4 scenarios, then you can benefit from applying the BUDGET ACCOUNT SYSTEM.   And, you *don't* even have to organize *most* of your spending. You'll be amazed at how simple the BUDGET ACCOUNT SYSTEM is. Read on!

2 Why Take a Psychological Approach to Personal Budgeting?

I am a psychologist. My experience as a psychologist has taught me that our financial life is as important to our emotional well-being as our career, our recreational life, our health and physical fitness, and our social and family life. My philosophy about financial matters can be partly expressed as follows:

Happiness and Satisfaction do not result from the amount of money we have or from the specific things we purchase, but rather from the sense of personal mastery which we can derive from managing our resources in an intelligent, reasoned fashion.

You've heard it all before:

"Save your money!"

"Put that money aside for when you really need it!"

"If you had just set some money aside for emergencies, you wouldn't be in that fix today!"

But somehow, you've never been shown a good way to save, put aside, and organize your money. So, the money isn't there when you need it, and sometimes you feel frustrated, deprived, and defeated when you run into financial troubles. Those are uncomfortable and even psychologically destructive emotions. And, with the use of a simple, easy-to-use system, you'll handle your finances so well that you won't have to experience those feelings. In this volume you will be shown, step by step, the BUDGET ACCOUNT method for organizing your finances. The method is not only easy—it is enjoyable. When you have employed it you will have feelings of control and mastery. You can have the feeling of self-esteem and competence that a well-organized approach to personal money management can give you.

Why Did a Psychologist Write this Book ?

In my twenty years of working in human services, I've seen and used many different approaches to human problems and issues. In developing my approach to helping people, I have been very much impressed by the importance of helping people at the level at which they need and want the help.

Some people can be helped at what we may call a practical and strategic level of intervention. (Personal budgeting is one example of a practical, strategic approach). At a somewhat deeper psychological level, some people need to be helped either to analyze their thoughts, work through their emotions, or examine their attitudes. And, at an even deeper psychological level, some people need to gain insight into how they became the persons they are today by examining their personal history, motivations, and needs. All three levels are valid, helpful approaches when skillfully used by a practitioner who applies them with the permission and understanding of the client.

Although I am currently working with clients at all three levels, I have been impressed by how often a practical, strategic approach will serve a client's needs. In this case, I am writing this volume in the hope that it will serve a number of readers' needs.

I'd like to recount a story which illustrates the way in which a psychologist can, in some instances, miss the boat by forgetting about the practical aspects of situations. This story was told by one of my graduate school professors, Dr. K.

> An elderly woman, who lived alone in her own home, had become depressed. She had lost some mobility, and was dependent on a wheel chair. She could no longer handle some of her own needs, such as food preparation, and therefore had to have help in her home. Since she had become depressed, a psychologist was trying to treat her depression with a typical form of verbal psychotherapy. The therapy was not helping to alleviate the depression, and Dr. K. was consulted. When Dr. K., a behavioral psychologist, analyzed the situation, she said, "This woman doesn't need a psychologist; she needs a carpenter." Eureka! A cabinet maker was employed. He took out the lower kitchen cabinets and built a new set, with a lower top and a recess beneath. With these renovations, the woman could pull her wheel chair right up to the counter and prepare her own food, make her own tea, etcetera. Her depression lifted.

The depressed woman in that illustration needed a redesigned kitchen, not psychotherapy. In my estimation, there are many situations in which the uncomfortable, perhaps even debilitating emotions which people experience can be remedied through strategic means. If a deeper exploration and intervention is needed, then psychotherapy may be undertaken, often with rewarding results. After all, psychotherapy very often is a remarkably helpful venture. And there need be no shame attached to requesting it.

However, some readers may be suffering frustration, anxiety, and low self-esteem due to a lack of skill or self-control in financial matters. And many can help themselves by applying the methods described here in this book. This book is written in the hope that the practical solutions inherent in the BUDGET ACCOUNT SYSTEM will give readers the means to end that discomfort and replace it with a sense of control and personal mastery. It can. Read on.

3 The Problem With Typical Budgeting Systems

Maybe you've read a magazine article or a book about personal money management. Many of those methods start by giving you this task: look back through all your personal financial records of the past year—your check books, savings accounts, credit card receipts, and any other receipts which you may have kept—and write down every dime you can account for. The idea is for you to figure out just where you have spent all your money for the past year.

Maybe it would be helpful for you to know how you spent every dime...BUT...who wants to figure it out? It would be a time-consuming, painstaking, aggravating task to go through all your records for a year to try to figure out where you spent every dime of your money. And, there is a risk. It might make you so sick and tired of the whole idea of budgeting that you'd give up in despair.

After suggesting that you go through the difficult process of analysis, the typical budgeting system then suggests that you determine the amount which you can afford to spend each month on certain expenses. There are often guidelines presented. For instance, it may be suggested that you set a limit for the amount of money you spend each month on going out for lunch. Theoretically, that's not a bad idea. *But, most persons don't want to keep track of exactly how much they've spent.* And, they don't want to feel limited. That doesn't mean people don't realize that they have to *be* limited; they just don't want to *feel* limited. And, they don't want to go through the detailed process of writing down the amount they spend on lunch every day. Let's face it: most of us just don't want to organize our lives and our finances in ways which feel too detailed, too tedious, and too constricting. Nora's story illustrates the problems with typical budgeting methods:

> I'm a "middle income" person, neither wealthy nor poor. When I got out of school and got a job, I figured I could do okay on my salary. I rented an apartment—a nice one, but nothing really expensive. I bought a two-year-old car, and took a bank loan for it. At the advice of a long-time family friend and financial advisor, I took out a whole life insurance policy and started an Individual Retirement Account. I didn't go bananas on clothes or vacations—you know, the way some young professionals get into really bad financial straits. I used my charge card quite a bit for restaurants and minor purchases, but I always paid enough to keep the balance under two hundred dollars. I did spend quite a lot on lunches and dinners in restaurants, and I always had a couple of bottles of wine on ice. But I thought I deserved it since it gave me pleasure and since otherwise I was pretty moderate in my spending.
>
> After a few trips to attend important family events and some car repairs, my credit card balance was over two thousand. I tried to get a handle on things but everything seemed so confusing! One month my checking account would be empty a week before payday. The next month I'd have a

cushion near the end of the month, and I'd loosen up a bit, and all of a sudden my car insurance and life insurance premiums would be due, the cushion would disappear, and I'd be at the bank getting a cash advance on my credit card. I just couldn't get a clear picture of where I was financially at any given moment. I was about to panic.

So, I bought a book on personal budgeting and read some magazine articles on it, and "I was really gung ho." I did what they said. I got out my check book and my credit card records and all the receipts I could find and I painstakingly analyzed all my spending habits. And I do mean painstaking! It took me three nights, but I finally got it all analyzed. Something had to give if I were going to be able to manage that occasional family trip and that occasional car repair. I just didn't have enough income for my lifestyle. I could see four possible ways to trim my expenses: 1) get a roommate; 2) drop the insurance and the Individual Retirement Account;   3) sell my car and rely on public transportation and taxis; and 4) cut way down on the restaurant eating. Having my own apartment and my own car are what make me feel like an independent adult, so there's no way I was going to give those up! And I'd have felt really super irresponsible dropping my insurance and my IRA. So, I made up my mind to cut way back on my restaurant eating.

I had everything budgeted, just like they said. Everything! When I got home at night I'd go over the day's spending. I had about 20 categories of expenses. I'd subtract what I spent on each of them from the monthly allotment. It felt like being in jail! And some of it was so stupid! I mean, like it's really going to help to write down every penny I spend on gasoline for the car! Writing it down isn't going to improve my car's gas mileage!

So now and then I'd rebel. I'd go to happy hour and dinner with friends from work. I'd just use the charge card and try to forget it. I hated feeling restricted! And I hated writing everything down like a persnickety little old accountant or something! (to be continued)

Nora's story gives you a good idea of a few things. It illustrates the problems with typical personal budgets. And it shows the feelings of confusion and rebellion which can result from an unsuccessful attempt to implement a budget. In Chapter 6 you will read the conclusion of Nora's story, after she has learned the author's BUDGET ACCOUNT SYSTEM.

4 Why Don't We Have a Good "Feel" for our Budgets?

"Regular" Expenses

"Regular" expenses are those which we have every month. So, our rent (or house payment) is a regular expense. Our utility bills are regular expenses. Buying groceries is a regular expense, as are gasoline for our car, toiletries, and buying a newspaper.

If all our expenses were regularly-occurring ones like these, we would probably develop a "feel" for our budget, and plan accordingly.

Intermittent, Occasional, and "Unpredictable" Expenses

What throws into disarray your ability to budget your money "by feel"? It's *not* the regularly-occurring expenses described above. The "monkey wrenches in the machinery" are the expenses which occur irregularly, occasionally, or "unpredictably." The reason I put the word "unpredictably" in quotes is that *they are not really unpredictable*. They just *feel* that way.

And just which expenses am I talking about? I'm talking about bills for automobile repair, automobile insurance, vacations, holiday gifts, life insurance premiums...that kind of thing. If these expenses were spread out evenly month-to-month, then you would not experience the "false build-ups" and the "quick drops" in your checking account which make your finances confusing. You would be able to come to terms with them along with your regular expenses. But they don't, and they throw the average person's financial awareness and planning into confusion.

Automobile Repair:
Just One Example of a Troublesome Intermittent Expense

Think about the following scenario, and see if it helps get across the idea of how intermittent expenses confuse our thinking:

> You're in a restaurant, sitting back with an after-dinner drink, having just savored shrimp cocktail, filet mignon, salad, and wine. And, best of all, you haven't spent a dime...yet. But, before you leave, you are handed a check with some big numbers on it.
>
> Before paying the check in the restaurant, you wouldn't kid yourself into thinking that you were eating for free, would you? And when the waiter hands you the check, you don't say **"Oh, no!! What a stroke of bad luck! A check to pay!"**

But, you may have a very similar reaction in other situations. Let's consider the example of auto repair. Say you've driven your car for the last 3 months without a single repair expense. You're saving money, right?...**WRONG ! !**

Almost all car repairs are the result of normal wear and tear, **not** bad luck. Since you've driven your car for 3 months, you're due for lubrication (oil, oil filter, and chassis lubrication). That's twenty dollars. And, while driving for 3 months, you've also used up approximately:

- $25 worth of your car's tires
- $12 worth of your car's exhaust system
- $17 worth of your car's brakes
- $ 5 worth of your car's battery
- $10 worth of your car's alternator and regulator
- $25 worth of your car's air conditioning system
- $ 1 worth of your car's thermostat
- $10 worth of your car's radiator and water pump
- $15 worth of your car's front end
- $15 worth of your car's clutch and/or transmission, and
- $10 worth of your car's carburetor.

That's $145. Add in the $20 for lubrication and $15 for incidentals, and we're at $180 for 3 months, an average of $60 per month. And, do you know something? That's a pretty good approximation of what it is costing you to keep your car repaired. Oh, yes, I know. You may have gone a year now with no repairs—just gasoline and lubrication. But eventually, some month, just when you least expect it...wham!!!! You're going to have auto repair expenses. It's inevitable. And six or seven hundred dollars worth of car repair expenses following a year of "good luck" would not be unusual.

Even if it's true, what's the point of all this?

A) It is true; and

B) Here's the point:

For the 12 months that you enjoy trouble-free driving, you may approach the end of each month with $60 left over. As you approach the end of the month, you "just feel okay financially." You look in your check book, and the balance "just seems pretty good for this time of month." So, with no expenses in sight, you indulge in any one of a number of luxuries (an extra dinner out, an article of clothing, an art print, an exquisite brand of scotch, a gift for a loved one, or tickets to a cultural or a sporting event). After enjoying your extra $60 per month for 12 months, you've spent 12 x $60 = $720. When you're "hit with the unexpected" car repair bill, you have to put it on a charge card. You worry about paying it off. And, just think of all the little bits of frustration you go through! First, when the car begins showing signs of trouble, you're anxious, knowing that a major expense may be at hand. Secondly, while the car is in the shop being looked at, you're anxious and tense awaiting the mechanic's diagnosis, because you know you'll have to charge the bill. And third, after paying the bill, you feel "put upon" and upset, and you're angry that your income doesn't quite meet your expenses.

I hope that this example regarding auto repair conveys to you how intermittent expenses throw off our ability to "budget by feel." And, I hope the example also convinces you of the enormous savings in terms of emotional energy which we can experience by effective budgeting.

5 Handling the Intermittent Expenses

One of the key concepts here is that almost all of us "go by feel" when it comes to budgeting. And, I'm *not* going to ask you to change that. I am convinced that with the addition of a simple system for handling intermittent expenses, you can "budget by feel," and do it successfully.

The Coffee Can Approach

Let's get back to the problem we had with the $720 car repair. Suppose we had an empty coffee can in a cupboard, with a label that read "auto repair." Suppose that every month after receiving our paycheck we put sixty dollars into the coffee can and told ourselves that it was to be used exclusively for that purpose. In that case, as we approached the end of each month, we may not have "felt so flush." By quickly looking over our checking account, we may **not** have felt okay about making the extra luxury expenditures described previously. As the cash built up to the seven hundred dollar mark during our 12 months of trouble-free driving, we may have been tempted to conclude that we were the beneficiaries of good luck, and that we could afford to spend some of our auto repair money on something else. But, if we had left the auto repair money alone, then when the repair bills did materialize, we'd have been ready. We would *not* have felt anxious, tense, and put-upon. In fact, we would have felt competent, clever, and responsible. This sense of mastery and of freedom from worry is worth a lot. And, you can have it without using a tedious, detailed budget system. Read on.

So Much For Car Repair.

Is There More?

Clearly, car repairs are not the only type of intermittent expense which can throw our "seat of the pants" calculations off. For instance, there's auto insurance. The amount of your auto insurance depends on how many vehicles you have insured, on the value of your car (comprehensive insurance) and your locale (liability insurance). You may pay your auto insurance once a year, twice a year, or even on some other payment schedule. Semi-annual premiums are pretty common, though. So, twice a year, just when you least expect it ...pow!! You're hit with an auto insurance bill of, say $270. Once again, there is potential here for finding ourselves short of money. Worse still, there is potential here for feeling incompetent, feeling impoverished, and feeling like a poor planner. In short, there is potential for feeling low self-esteem. Since a $270 semi-annual premium, divided by 6, equals $45, the needed expenditure amounts to an average of $45 per month. And, if we had set aside $45 per month (in a coffee can labelled "auto insurance") we would have "felt less wealthy" by $45 per month, and we may have just naturally, without tedious planning, eased our spending by $45 per month to accommodate. Then, when the insurance bill arrived, we would not have felt uncomfortable, destructive emotions. In fact, we would once again have looked into our coffee can, smiled, and felt a sense of mastery.

In a Way, I'm Just Kidding

It's time to tell you, before I fill out the entire example with the coffee can bit, that it's just that: a bit—an analogy. Oh, the concept is real, and what I'm going to suggest that you do is the equivalent of using coffee cans. But I'm going to recommend something much more sophisticated and useful. Keep that in mind as I finish describing the technique with the coffee can analogy.

The important idea is for you to: 1) estimate most of your intermittent expenses, 2) calculate what the expense is on a monthly basis, and 3) set aside the appropriate amount of funds for each expense at the beginning of the month. That way, as you progress through the month, there will be no "false build-ups" and no "quick drops" due to intermittent expenses. When you "get a feel" for your financial position, your "feel" may be an accurate one. The unpleasant surprises which might otherwise throw you into disarray will be taken care of:

Let's say that you have identified the following intermittent expenses:

1. vacations
2. auto repair
3. auto insurance
4. life insurance and disability income insurance
5. organization dues
6. home furnishings.

1. VACATION: Suppose you like to take two vacations per year.

You take one during the Summer and one during the holidays. Perhaps you like to spend $400 - $500 for each vacation.

$450 x 2 = $900/12 months = $75 per month.

2. AUTO REPAIR: Let's say you have a car that is more than 2 years old, and that you agree with my estimate of $720 per year for repairs. $720/12 months = $60 per month.

3. AUTO INSURANCE: Assume you make two semi-annual payments of $270 each. $270 x 2 = $540/12 months = $45 per month.

4. LIFE INSURANCE AND DISABILITY INCOME INSURANCE:

   Let's say you have a life insurance policy with an annual premium of $280 and a disability income insurance policy with an annual premium of $200. $280 + $200 = $480/12 months = $40 per month.

5. ORGANIZATION DUES: Assume you belong to a club or organization with annual dues of $120. $120/12 months = $10 per month.

6. HOME FURNISHINGS: Let's say you'd like to have a few hundred dollars every now and then to buy something for your home (a toaster oven, a gas grille, a reclining chair, a radial arm saw, etcetera). If you were to set aside $20 per month, it would give you $240 per year to put toward such purchases.

THE ALLOCATION

Thus, here's what you've got for a monthly allotment to a budget account:

1.	Vacation	$75/month
2.	Auto repair	$60/month
3.	Auto insurance	$45/month
4.	Life and disability income insurance	$40/month
5.	Organization Dues	$10/month
6.	Home furnishings	<u>$20/month</u>
	TOTAL	$250/month

Now we've selected a number of intermittent expenses to budget for, and we've predicted the monthly average of these expenses. In Chapter 6 we'll discuss the way to actually set up the BUDGET ACCOUNT.

A Note about Payroll Schedules

In this book, I will be illustrating personal budgeting problems and solutions. And, in doing so, I will be making an implicit assumption that you receive regular income on a once per month basis. Obviously, many of my readers will be in different situations. Some of you may be paid 24 times per year, on the 1st and 16th of every month. Some of you may be paid every two weeks, which means that you receive 26 paychecks per year (and, once every 11 years you will have a "27 paycheck year"). Some of you may be self-employed, and may receive payment from your customers on a less predictable basis. And, some of you may be retired and may live on a combination of monthly pension checks and quarterly dividends.

It will be impossible for me to write everything five times to accommodate these five different schedules of receiving your income. I have worked on the personal budgeting circumstances of persons with different income schedules and am confident that, with some thought, you can translate the suggestions in this book to fit your own particular circumstance.

6 Setting up a BUDGET ACCOUNT

(NO KIDDING THIS TIME)

I told you I that in a way I was just kidding about the coffee cans. Here's what I really recommend:

> Find a bank or a savings and loan which offers a good deal on checking accounts. How good a deal you can get depends in part on where you live. But, in most locations the banking market is competitive enough that you should be able to get checking accounts in which you will be charged no activity fee as long as you keep a reasonable minimum balance (perhaps $250 or $500). And, you should be able to find checking accounts which will pay you interest if you maintain a high enough average daily balance.

> After finding your bank, open up TWO CHECKING ACCOUNTS. Yes. Two. This isn't foolish...just organized. Call one of those accounts your "regular account." Deposit your paychecks into it, and use it for your typical daily or monthly needs, such as checks for your rent or mortgage, utilities, athletic club fees, grocery bills, etc. Call the other account your "BUDGET ACCOUNT." This BUDGET ACCOUNT will be the subject of much of the following discussion. Your budget account will help you keep your finances organized. It will help you

keep your financial anxieties minimized. It will help you keep your self-esteem and your feelings of personal mastery high. Read on.

Any bank will allow you certain privileges. One privilege is that by filling out a form you can instruct the bank to transfer funds from one account to another on a certain day of each month. What you do is instruct the bank to transfer your allocated $250 FROM YOUR "REGULAR ACCOUNT" TO YOUR "BUDGET ACCOUNT" every month on the 10th of the month. Why the 10th? That's arbitrary. It could as easily be any other day.

Then, every month, you first go to your checking account registers and subtract $250 from your "regular account" balance and add $250 to your "BUDGET ACCOUNT" balance. And, you keep track of your balance in each of your six separate accounts. I will show you how to do so, using six sheets of paper in a looseleaf notebook. (Or, you could use a computer spreadsheet program if you have one. But pencil, paper, and a looseleaf notebook will be fine). You account for the $250 by noting SIX automatic deposits into each of the SIX accounts you've set up :

1. vacation $75
2. auto repair $60
3. auto insurance $45
4. life & disability income insurance $40
5. organization dues $10
6. home furnishings $20
   TOTAL $250

As far as the bank is concerned, your BUDGET ACCOUNT is ONE ACCOUNT. But, *as far as you are concerned...*

> IT IS ACTUALLY SIX SEPARATE ACCOUNTS, AND YOU TREAT THEM AS SEPARATE JUST AS THOUGH THEY WERE DOLLAR BILLS KEPT IN SIX COFFEE CANS.

At the beginning, it may take some self-discipline to resist using the funds in these accounts for something other than their designated use.   But, after you have experienced the feelings of mastery and self-esteem that come from being organized in this way, you will be very highly motivated to keep the funds separate.   It won't take self-discipline or willpower for long. It will be natural for you.

Here is the conclusion of Nora's story, begun in Chapter 3:

> Then I found out about the BUDGET ACCOUNT SYSTEM. The bottom line is about the same for me, but it's so much simpler! Incredibly easier! Now I no longer set budget limits for anything I pay for every month, like rent, phone, food, gasoline, restaurant eating, and utilities. The only budgeted items are the unexpected ones: car repair, car insurance, life insurance, IRA contributions, and travel. For each of those expenses I divide the yearly cost by 12 and put that much aside every month. What that does that's so incredible is that my checkbook balance makes sense now. I look at it and I know right where I am. After I pay the rent, make a credit card payment, and set aside money for the unexpected things I mentioned, my balance just slides down gradually, and I can sort of

"judge it by feel." I've set a goal of ending each month with $200 in my checking account.

If I'm under, say...$300 on the 20th of the month, I know I have to go easy. I still can't eat in restaurants too often, and when I do I order carefully and I drink water. The thing is, it's not a confusing mess anymore. I don't mind cutting back when I know exactly where the careful spending will leave me. In fact, I like it. It gives me a sense of control over things. When I get a raise, I'll keep my BUDGET ACCOUNT going. Even though I'll have a lot more money, I'll still keep things in line. I'll still aim for a $200 check book balance at the end of the month, and then I'll decide how to spend or invest anything over the $200. I love the sense of control!

We've now explained and illustrated how to set up a BUDGET ACCOUNT. In Chapter 7, we'll look at some hypothetical examples of some budget account transactions. We will show you exactly what your balance sheets will look like.

7 Some Examples

AN HYPOTHETICAL EXAMPLE OF AN AUTO REPAIR ACCOUNT

Take a look at Appendix 1 on page 99. It is an hypothetical example of about five months of BUDGET ACCOUNT activity in auto repair. Notice that the recording sheets for keeping track of accounts have the following features:

1. A place to name the account.

2. A place to note the amount of the monthly allocation, and the month and year it went into effect.

3. A column for the date of transactions.

4. A column for a brief description of transactions.

5. A column for credits (deposits).

6. A column for debits (checks written or transfers made to other "accounts").

7. A column for the balance.

First, notice that the person (call her Les) is allocating $50 per month for auto repair. Then, notice that on 4-10-86 Les credits the account for $150 in an "initial deposit." (This is the point at which Les has first opened up her budget account. Later, in the chapter on "Helpful Hints for Opening a Budget Account," we'll discuss the appropriate amount to allocate as an initial deposit).

On May 10, Les records an automatic deposit ("auto dep") bringing her balance to $200. Then, on May 24, she has to write check #101 to Athens Auto Air for an evaporator and drier. This withdrawal of $102.78 leaves a balance of $97.22. On June 10, an "auto dep" of fifty dollars brings the balance to $147.22. And on June 14, Les writes check #105 to Ace's Garage for a tune-up. The account balance is down to $88.07. July 10 and August 10 see "auto deps" bringing the account balance to $188.07. Then, at the end of August, Les is "hit with two auto repair expenses" totaling over $140. But, she doesn't feel "hit." She calmly and confidently writes out checks 112 and 114 to Sears and to Athens Bandag for a battery and 2 new tires respectively. The two withdrawals bring the account balance to $45.62— low, but not depleted. September sees an auto dep of $50 and a minor repair ($24.50) at Ace's Garage, leaving the account with $71.12.

And so it goes. As long as Les continues to automatically credit her auto repair account with $50 per month, she will very likely have enough to cover all her auto repair bills. Think of the peace of mind and freedom from unnecessary worry that this gives her. Les may run into an eight, ten, or even twelve month period of no auto repairs other than routine maintenance. She may therefore build up an apparent excess of auto repair funds—perhaps $400 to $600. And, she may be tempted to believe that she has "really lucked out," and may want to transfer some of her auto repair funds to another account. But it will probably be in her better interest to leave the auto repair funds in the account they were intended for. Because someday she may face a really large auto repair bill, such as a major engine overhaul. Then instead of worrying about how to pay for it, she'll have the funds. And, instead of an agonizing internal debate about whether the old car is worth putting money into, she can just get the car repaired, confident in her knowledge that her car is costing her only fifty dollars per month to maintain.

AN HYPOTHETICAL EXAMPLE
OF A VACATION ACCOUNT

Take a look at Appendix 2 on page 100. It is an hypothetical example of eight months of budget account activity in a VACATION account. The recording sheet has the same features as the AUTO REPAIR account recording sheet which we have already looked at.

First of all, notice that the budgeter, Chris, has decided in April of 1986 to make a monthly deposit of $75 to VACATION, and has begun with an initial deposit of $225. In May, June, and July, Chris makes "auto deps" of $75 each, to build the VACATION account to $450. Then, Chris decides to take a Summer vacation. When he purchases airline tickets from the travel agency on July 15, he simply writes a check for $159 and debits his BUDGET ACCOUNT accordingly, leaving a balance of $291. Then, on July 19, Chris buys $200 worth of travelers checks from a bank, again writing a check from his BUDGET ACCOUNT check book, and debiting his VACATION account accordingly, leaving a balance of $91. Then Chris goes on vacation, and spends his $200 in travelers checks, and spends even more, using a charge card. Notice that the August and September "auto deps" bring the VACATION account to $241. Then, when his charge card comes due, he totals up all the charges which are attributable to his vacation, and writes a check for $150 to his credit card, debiting the account. Then, we see that Chris' October, November, and December "auto deps" bring his VACATION account back up over $300, which we imagine he may use for a holiday vacation.

Let's talk a little more about the concept of using BUDGET ACCOUNT checks to help pay off charge cards. In the above example, we see that Chris wrote a check for $150 to pay a credit card balance. But, that may not have been the entire balance. Chris may be in the habit of paying for his routine gasoline purchases with his credit card, and he pays those credit card balances with checks from his REGULAR CHECKING ACCOUNT. In this example, Chris may have had a credit card balance of $182, of which $32 were routine gasoline purchases and $150 were vacation expenses. He may have written two checks, one from his REGULAR ACCOUNT for $32 and one from his BUDGET ACCOUNT for $150, for a total of $182. The bank doesn't care how many checks you enclose in the envelope; they're only interested in the total. So, as a convenience, you can use your credit card for purchases, and can write the checks and make the appropriate BUDGET ACCOUNT debits later.

8 Temporary Accounts

So far we have discussed two hypothetical examples of BUDGET ACCOUNT categories: auto repair and vacation. Both types of accounts are permanent. That is, you may maintain a running account of your debits and credits in these areas for years; and, in fact, I hope you will. However, your BUDGET ACCOUNT can have another use. You can establish temporary accounts to help you to set aside funds received from some specific source, so that you can control your expenditures from that source. This will give you increased satisfaction in your use of this money.

By now, I hope you realize immediately that when I write "You can establish temporary accounts," I'm not suggesting that you go to the bank and open still another checking account. I'm suggesting that you can deposit the money into your existing BUDGET ACCOUNT, and you can get out a new recording sheet, entitle it, and record the deposit.

AN HYPOTHETICAL EXAMPLE OF A TEMPORARY ACCOUNT USED TO MANAGE THE DISBURSEMENT OF AN INCOME TAX REFUND

Let's take a look at Appendix 3 on page 101. This is an example of an account set up on a temporary basis to help you to have a sense of control over your use of a particular sum of money. Why would someone set up such a temporary account?

Have you ever received some money from a source other than your usual income? Of course you have. Possibilities include a) a tax refund; b) a cash gift from a relative; c) payment to you for "moonlighting" work; or d) proceeds from the sale of a possession. Perhaps you remember saying "Great! Now I can use this money for a special purpose." You deposited this extra money into your regular checking account. But, when the time came for you to use the money for your special purpose, it had been "absorbed" into your cash flow. It had been used for typical expenses, and now that you were ready to use it for the special purpose, you could no longer truly identify any extra money. What could you do? Either you abandoned the special purpose, and felt disappointed or cheated, or you made the expenditure anyway, but fell behind financially. You certainly did *not* get a feeling of satisfaction from having saved the funds for the special purpose and for having used them that way.

A temporary account in your BUDGET ACCOUNT can solve this problem for you, just as it did for Sam, who set up the temporary account shown in Appendix 3 on page 101. On May 29, 1987, Sam received a federal income tax refund. He promptly put the money into his budget account, and credited it to a new, temporary account, called "Temporary Account for Handling 1986 Tax Refund."

Sam had a few "special purposes" for his tax refund dollars: 1. He wanted to take an extra vacation trip; 2. He wanted to buy himself a set of new stereo speakers; and 3. He wanted to make a small investment in collectibles. As you can see, on August 3 he wrote a check for $386 for airfare for his vacation, leaving a balance of $266. On September 22 he wrote a check for $100 for cash to be used to purchase collectibles, leaving $166. Then, sometime in October, he used his credit card to purchase a set of stereo speakers for $166 or more. And, on November 20 he wrote a check for the balance of his temporary account—$166—to help pay off the charge card for the purchase.

Sam can look back at his use of his income tax refund with a sense of personal satisfaction. When he received the refund, he immediately had ideas as to its use. Then he put the funds aside, as surely as if he had hidden cash in a cookie jar. When the opportunities came to use the money for his special purposes, it was right there waiting. No muss, no fuss, no bother! Just a sense of being organized...of being competent ...of being in control. You can do it, too!

You've now been shown how to set up a budget account. You've been shown how to decide on amounts of money to set aside for specific purposes on a regular basis. And, you've been shown how to set up a temporary account to help you save and disburse extra money. In Chapter 9 we'll consider some helpful hints for getting started on this adventure.

9

Some Helpful Hints for Opening a BUDGET ACCOUNT

1. Deciding on Your Monthly Allocations

Make a list of categories of intermittent expenses for which you would like to allocate money on a regular basis. Use the worksheet in Appendix 4 on page 102. List the categories of expenses in the lefthand column. Then, notice the FIVE columns, all with the same heading: "monthly amount." There are FIVE of them so you can experiment with the amounts. Write in an amount for each expense in the first column. Add them up, and enter the sum in the "total" line at the bottom. Then, juggle those figures around a bit until you're satisfied that they're reasonable.

2. Determining the Size of Initial Deposits

Give some thought to the appropriate size of your initial deposit to each individual account. In the case of some accounts, your initial deposit may simply be the amount which you will allocate monthly. For instance, suppose you are establishing a "home furnishings" account, and you have decided on a monthly allocation of $20. An initial deposit of $20 is appropriate. You will put these funds toward an item of home furnishing when the funds are there.

The case of automobile repair, however, is another story. After all, you do not typically decide on spending money for an auto repair the way you decide on spending for a couch. Assuming that you consider it a necessity to have your car running, when a need for a repair arises, you *must* make the expenditure. And, at the moment when you decide to start your BUDGET ACCOUNT, you may have no way of knowing whether or not an auto repair is imminent. How, then, can you decide on the size of a reasonable initial deposit?

It would probably be reasonable to initially deposit three or four months' worth of deposits into an auto repair account. Of course, if your car is less than two years old and is under a manufacturer's warranty, you may begin with as little as your regular one month allocation.

In the case of auto insurance, calculate your initial deposit by multiplying the number of months until your next premium payment is due *times* one-twelfth of your annual premium, and then subtracting the total of automatic deposits you will make from now until the month of the premium due date. For example, if your auto insurance premiums are $540 per year, then your monthly expense is 540/12 = $45. If your next premium payment is a semi-annual payment due on August 20, then you will want your August 10 "auto dep" to bring your balance to a minimum of $270. If you open your BUDGET ACCOUNT in April, you will be making 4 more automatic deposits by the premium due date (May, June, July, and August auto deps). Those 4 auto deps will total $180. Therefore, you will want an initial deposit of $270 minus $180, or $90 which, coupled with your 4 subsequent deposits of $180, will cover your payment.

3. Posting Interest and Check-Printing Charges

As long as you find a bank with favorable checking account privileges, you will probably not encounter any monthly service charges, and hopefully you will be paid interest. You will, of course, have to pay to have checks printed. A question therefore arises: "How should I post check-printing charges and interest?"

Pick ONE account as the one *into* which you will deposit interest and *from* which you will deduct the fee for having checks printed. I myself use my VACATION account for this purpose. I find it to be particularly rewarding to see my VACATION ACCOUNT increase as a result of my BUDGET ACCOUNT SYSTEM.

The issue of interest raises one other point. Even a person of moderate means may end up having a typical BUDGET ACCOUNT balance of three-to-ten thousand dollars. This could mean annual interest of $500, or even more. And interest income is, of course, taxable income. If you believe that your BUDGET ACCOUNT interest will affect your April 15 payment, then you may wish to put one-third of your monthly interest into a "TAX ESCROW account." Thus, if you receive monthly interest of $24, you could choose to post an $8 credit to your tax escrow account and a $16 credit to your vacation account. You would then be secure in knowing, while on vacation, that you weren't spending money which you would later have to pay back to the Internal Revenue Service.

This account will also be very helpful for you if you sometimes receive income from which no income tax is withheld (e.g. capital gains, payment for consulting work, etcetera). The concept of a "tax escrow account" will be discussed more fully in Chapter 10, "Sixteen Possible Uses for a BUDGET ACCOUNT."

4. Managing Income from Sources Other Than Salary

When you receive funds from a source other than your regular income, decide which account or accounts to credit, and *put the funds into your BUDGET ACCOUNT.* If you prefer, establish a temporary account with which to plan and monitor your use of these funds. Do not just deposit extra funds into your regular account and take the risk that they will be "absorbed" without your having any sense of mastery over the process.

In a previous section, we illustrated the use to which "Sam" put $652 received as an income tax refund. Remember the author's philosophy of the BUDGET ACCOUNT SYSTEM:

Happiness and Satisfaction do not result from the amount of money we have or from the specific things we purchase, but rather from the sense of personal mastery which we can derive from managing our resources in an intelligent, reasoned fashion.

5. Managing "Start - up Problems"

Don't lose heart if you run into some difficulty during the early stages of your BUDGET ACCOUNT program ! ! For instance, you may open your budget account, and then immediately encounter a large auto repair expense. If you have to charge the expense, **do so**. Then make payments on it from your auto repair account as those funds become available.

Some persons being instructed in the use of the BUDGET ACCOUNT SYSTEM have encountered just such a situation. They have said, "I'm paying 18% interest on my charge card, and I have the money in the BUDGET ACCOUNT sitting there earning only five-and-one-half percent interest. Wouldn't it be better for me to just empty out the BUDGET ACCOUNT to pay the repair bill, and then start the BUDGET ACCOUNT up again later?"

My answer: No!! In the **short term,** it's true that there is an interest rate differential. But, in the **long term,** your use of the BUDGET ACCOUNT SYSTEM is so valuable that keeping it intact is **well worth** that interest differential in the short term. Fred's story will probably communicate this more effectively:

My finances used to be a mess. And it's not that I had an irresponsible attitude. It's that "I didn't have any method to my madness." I'd sometimes get really strict with myself for awhile. You know, no beer except what I'd buy in a market...bring my lunch to work...only go to a movie theatre if it was a dollar or a dollar-and-a-half for admission. Then after that nickel-and-dime belt-tightening for a few weeks, I'd go out and buy a radial arm saw for $300.

My roommate Jim was the same way. We both went to a class and learned about the BUDGET

ACCOUNT SYSTEM. And, we each set up the exact same BUDGET ACCOUNT. We put $200 a month aside like this:

travel	$50
car repair	$40
car insurance	$50
hobbies and tools	$35
holiday gifts	$25
T O T A L	$200

We started out with $200 as a first deposit. Neither of us had enough spare cash to make a bigger first deposit to auto repair or anything. Well, it looked like it was going to work out great for both of us. Then, it looked like it would be a flop for us both. Jim's Mom had to have surgery, and he had to make two trips out-of-state. He was too nervous to drive, so he flew. $600. My truck all-of-a-sudden needed rings and valves. $600. It was a real coincidence. We both got hit with a $600 bill when he only had $100 tucked away for it in his travel account and I only had $80 in my auto repair account.

Well, Jim said it was stupid to let a $400 account sit there getting almost no interest when he'd be paying 18 percent interest to leave it all on a charge card. So, he closed out his BUDGET ACCOUNT, and said he'd open it up again when he had the money. Me, I'd heard what Dr. Slavit suggested, and it made sense to me. So, I paid $80 up front for the truck engine overhaul. I put

$520 on a plastic card, and I kept my BUDGET ACCOUNT going.

You know, that BUDGET ACCOUNT is really fun. I only write 2 or 3 checks on it in a month, typically. It's really easy to keep track of it. Anyway, here's what I do. I keep a minimum balance of $300 in my "regular checking account." Every month I've been trying to cut back on expenses, and at the end of the month I write out 2 checks to my credit card. I write out one for $40 from my BUDGET ACCOUNT, and I write out one for every penny that I've got over $300 from my regular account. So, if I end up the month with $370 in my regular account, I send in a total of $110. It's working. It's been 3 months since the truck repair, and the next check will do it. The BUDGET ACCOUNT really gives me a way to keep everything under my thumb.

Jim, he's frustrated. Oh, his Mom's okay now, by the way. But he hasn't got the charge card paid off yet, and he hasn't re-opened his BUDGET ACCOUNT. Without the BUDGET ACCOUNT to help him keep things so he can see them, he just hasn't got the incentive that I've had to cut back on expenses and get things paid off. So for me, paying off the charge card slowly, interest and all, was worth it because the BUDGET ACCOUNT works.

10 Sixteen Possible Uses for a BUDGET ACCOUNT

The number and types of uses for a budget account are essentially limited only by your imagination. You'll be able to choose four, five, or six of the sixteen ways which I will describe here to give you a start. Describing the sixteen uses will illustrate the system for you even more, and will stimulate your imagination about other uses.

1. Investment in Financial Assets

Let's suppose you want to buy interest-paying bonds, which may cost approximately $1000 each if they sell near par value. But suppose also that you never have a free $1000 to invest. If you put $100 per month into a BUDGET ACCOUNT allocated for investment, every ten months you'll have $1000, and you can buy a bond. In this way, you can save money to buy bonds, stocks, or any other investment.

2. Paying Insurance Premiums

Let's assume that twice per year you're "hit with" semi-annual automobile insurance premiums of $260, and that once per year you're "slammed with" a $320 life insurance premium. That's $840 per year. If you set aside $70 per month in a BUDGET ACCOUNT allocated for insurance, you will never feel "slammed" by the "premium due" notice, because your money will be right there waiting.

3. Automobile Repair

If you feel upset when your car needs repair, and if you find yourself hoping to "avoid the bad luck" of auto repairs, then the BUDGET ACCOUNT can help you experience it differently. In Chapter 5, entitled "Why don't we have a good feel for our budgets?" I discussed the auto repair situation in detail. If you were to set aside $60 per month in a BUDGET ACCOUNT allocated for auto repairs, then even $720 worth of repair bills per year could be handled without discomfort.

4. Vacation Expenses

Many people forego vacations due to their expense. Many others go on vacation, but find that it takes them a long time to pay off the debt which they place on credit cards. If you want to take two vacations per year—perhaps one during the Summer and one during the holidays—and to spend between $400 and $500 per vacation, you'll need approximately $900 per year. Allocating $75 per month to a BUDGET ACCOUNT will result in that money being right there waiting. You'll enjoy the vacations much more, too, because of the increased peace of mind.

Valerie's experiences should make this point:

I used to go on vacation, even though I hadn't saved up for it. I'd use plastic cards. After all, if I'm not worth it to me, who is? But I'd worry about paying off the debt. So, listen to this. I'd go to the beach, right? And I'd get a motel room facing the ocean, right? Then after one night either I'd switch to a less expensive room, not facing the ocean, or I'd stay for the view but not enjoy the view 'cause I'd feel so guilty about the cost! What awful feelings!

That's not all. I love eating dinner in nice seafood restaurants. And I like wine with dinner. So there I'd be, and even though I'd be drooling over something on the menu for $18, I'd make myself order something for $12 even though I wasn't thrilled with it. And, either I'd skip the wine, or I'd order one glass of the cheapest one. Why? You know! The whole vacation would be like that. Either I'd deny myself something enjoyable to cut down on my credit charges, or I'd charge it and feel guilty. It wasn't worth it, believe me!

Now, it's different. I not only put $90 a month into my BUDGET ACCOUNT for vacation, but I put the interest into my vacation account as well. As long as I meet my financial obligations, I don't feel a shred of guilt about allocating so much for vacations. And, I *do* meet my financial obligations, partly because with my BUDGET ACCOUNT handling my intermittent expenses, it's easy for me to know exactly what I can and can't afford. When it's a little tight by the middle of the month, I cut back here and there. You know, no clothing purchases. No new magazine subscriptions. It's easy to cut back when you can see the results of cutting back, and when you've got something to work toward. And I've got my vacations to work toward. So cutting back on expenses feels purposeful, not constricting.

So anyway, when I'm ready to leave for vacation, I use my BUDGET ACCOUNT to buy a few hundred dollars worth of travelers checks. They're all paid for. No debt. No guilt. When I'm on vacation, if I want to order the most expensive dish on the menu, I do. As long as I have the travelers checks to pay for it, I know I'm being responsible. What a difference! And you've read what I wrote about the experiences I used to have! I thought I was emotionally disturbed! I was afraid I'd never be able to enjoy a vacation! I mean, *really* enjoy it with no guilt feelings or anything. It was a psychologist who taught me to beat the problem. But all he did was teach me a strategy: the BUDGET ACCOUNT SYSTEM.

5. Paying Membership Dues

Perhaps you're a member of a club, union, or professional association. Or maybe you hold a license in your occupation. And maybe these memberships and licenses cost you money. So, two or three times a year, "just when you least expect it". . .pow! One of them "puts the bite on you" for an annual membership fee. Even if your memberships and licenses add up to an average of $240 per year, a monthly allocation of $20 in a BUDGET ACCOUNT will mean that you'll have the money right there waiting.

6. Home Furnishings or Luxury Items

Perhaps you'd like to enhance the attractiveness or function of your home now and then with a new piece of furniture, or an original oil painting, or a microwave oven, stereo cassette deck, or radial arm saw. And, if you've found that you're not able to make such expenditures and feel okay about doing it, then a BUDGET ACCOUNT may help. Decide on a yearly amount of money which is realistic for you to allocate for this type of purchase. Even a moderate monthly allocation of $25 will give you a $300 purchase in a year. And, this account may be the one to which you would like to credit extra money which may come in via tax refunds, consultation fees, royalties, gifts, or the proceeds of a garage sale.

7. The "Night on the Town"

Let's assume that you really enjoy the luxury of an occasional expensive evening out, with a play or concert, elegant dining, and wine. (By the way, this may be the very type of expense which you may have to forego in order to have enough money to allocate for your BUDGET ACCOUNT). Perhaps you indulge in this type of luxury now and then, only to later feel guilty and worry that you've left yourself short for the next blast of insurance premiums, car repairs, organizational dues, etcetera.

If indeed you do want to treat yourself to an occasional expensive "night on the town," then make a monthly allocation into your BUDGET ACCOUNT for that purpose. A $15 monthly allocation will give you a $90 night out twice a year. This does not mean that you can't do it more often, if you have the money. It just allows you to do it occasionally with no resulting debts, and with more comfort and justification (just like Valerie and her vacation experiences).

8. The "$250 deductible" Account

You probably have a few types of insurance policies which have a "deductible" feature. That is, you are responsible for the first $100, $200, or $250 of a loss which you suffer. The "comprehensive" (collision, fire and theft) insurance policy on your car is a good example. Your homeowner's insurance policy, and possibly even your health insurance probably also have "a deductible."

Another way to look at the "deductible," feature is to say that you are "self-insured" for the first $250 (or whatever the amount is) of loss. And, by the way, you can probably "insure yourself" more cheaply for that $250 than the insurance company will. Policies with "no deductible" are much more expensive.

A $10 monthly allocation to your BUDGET ACCOUNT would give you your $250 after two years and one month. In this way you could cover one casualty loss *every* 25 months. And, if the account were to build up to more than the $250 "self-insurance fund," you could transfer the surplus to an account of your choice (e.g. home furnishings, vacation, night on the town, or investment in financial assets).

9. Income Tax Escrow Account

If you have income from sources other than payroll, then you may have a rather unpleasant surprise around April

15. Your taxable income includes almost all income, not just payroll, from which income taxes have been withheld. As part of your BUDGET ACCOUNT, you could have a tax escrow account. If your income tax rate is 28 percent, for example, you could take 28 percent of any extra income and deposit it into your BUDGET ACCOUNT, crediting your "tax escrow account." Then, you can use the remaining 72 percent of that income any way you wish. And, you can do so with more peace of mind, knowing that you've already prepared yourself for April 15.

10. Dream Boat Account

You may literally have a dream about buying a boat. But, you may have despaired about ever having the money available to do so. The BUDGET ACCOUNT SYSTEM allows you to begin saving for it in small amounts. Even a very small monthly allocation toward your dream boat will keep you from feeling immobilized in terms of that dream. As your small monthly deposits begin to add up, your hopes about ultimately fulfilling the dream will increase. Once you have the dream boat account, you will be more motivated to save on other expenses in order to put extra money into the account.

Just as with an "investment in financial assets account," funds from your dream boat account can be used to buy stocks, bonds, precious metals, collectibles, or any other investment which you hope will grow into amounts which will help you make your dream purchase. In Budget Account Use #12 ahead, you'll read about how Dave used his BUDGET ACCOUNT to save and invest for a new car. You could save and invest for a dream boat, a dream vacation home, etcetera, in the same way.

11. Holiday Gift Account

You may enjoy buying gifts for family, friends, and colleagues at the time of the holidays, but most people do not set aside funds for these gift purchases. They therefore must use available cash, plus credit cards. Sally was one such person. Here is her story:

I would always start out the holiday season with good intentions. First I'd write out a list of the persons I'd be buying gifts for. Then I'd decide on a total dollar amount I could afford. And last, I'd decide how much I could afford to spend on each person. It felt pretty weird, saying "I can spend $25 on Dad, but I can only spend $15 on Sis." Anyway, I'd stick to the plan 'til about a week before the holiday. Then I'd get "cold feet." I'd think I was being too cheap.

So, I'd get out the old charge card to buy one—just one—extravagant gift for someone. Then, it was as if a dam had burst. I'd buy a whole bunch of extravagant gifts, joyously charging them all. After the holiday, I'd look at my charge card bill. . .and I'd think back on seeing people open their gifts... and I'd realize that what they really appreciated was that I thought of them and bought them a gift. That the gift was extravagant didn't seem to mean anything. Now that I have a BUDGET ACCOUNT, it's all different. I set aside $25 each month, which gives me $300 in all. When the holidays come, it's enough to buy some pretty good gifts. And, I can stay within that $300 limit easily. It's so much better this way.

There's no reason why you can't do as Sally did, and set aside a certain amount of money each month for holiday gifts. You can always add money from current funds if you want to and if you have enough. Best of all, you'll really enjoy your holiday shopping even more, knowing that you've systematically set aside the money to finance it.

12. New Car Account

We've discussed at length the way to allocate funds to keep your used car running. But we have not yet discussed using the BUDGET ACCOUNT to save for a new car. Let's hear from Dave:

> I have a reliable used car. It's a 1978 Honda Accord. I've been using my BUDGET ACCOUNT to maintain it since 1986. In 1987, though, when the car was 9 years old, I realized that new car prices were getting very high. I knew I'd have to save up a sizeable down payment if I ever wanted to afford a new car. But, I hardly had any money left over after expenses. I figured I'd use my BUDGET ACCOUNT to start up a "new car account," and I had to start small. In 1987, I embarked on a "six year plan" to save money for a new car. My plan was to use my BUDGET ACCOUNT to maintain my car until it reached the age of 14 years, and then to replace it.

> I started with a monthly deposit of $25. I used to joke about it with my friends. After the first year, I'd tell them I had "$300 saved up for a new car." The plan was to increase my monthly savings by $50 each year. The original plan, then, looked like this:

Year	Monthly deposit	Yearly allocation	Balance at year's end
'87	$25	$300	$ 300
'88	$75	$900	$1200
'89	$125	$1500	$2700
'90	$175	$2100	$4800
'91	$225	$2700	$7500
'92	$275	$3300	$10800

That's right. My plan was to save for 6 years, and to have $10,800 ready for a new car purchase at the end of 1992. I figured that if I were lucky enough to have a balance in my "auto repair" account when the time came, I would shift that money into my "auto insurance" account, since my comprehensive auto insurance will go up when I get a newer car.

I followed my plan in '87 and '88, saving a total of $1200. But, I didn't get a good raise in '88, so I had to stay with $75 per month in '89, and then I was only able to go to $100 per month in '90. At the end of '89 I had $2100, and by October of '90 I had $3100. Then, I took a chance. I don't know if you remember this, but from August to October in 1990, the Dow Jones Industrial average fell from just a tad below 3000 to under 2400. When it fell under 2400, I used my entire "new car" account of $3100 and bought 100 shares of Xerox stock. I guess you know about the big stock market rally that started around the beginning of the Persian Gulf War.

When Xerox stock hit $55 dollars a share, I sold it, and netted $5400 on the sale (plus, I had received a dividend of $75). That meant I had made a capital gain of $2300. I put $725 into a new account ("Tax Escrow") and I put the $4675 plus the $75 dividend back into my "new car account." I'm still only putting $100 per month into my new car account, but by the end of March of '91 I had $5250 in the account, which is just about in line with my original plan. It was really exciting to make that "score" on Xerox. If it hadn't been for my "new car account" within my BUDGET ACCOUNT, I wouldn't have had the money to do it. When I eventually buy my new car, I'll have the satisfaction of knowing just what my stock market adventure did for me. My BUDGET ACCOUNT is working out incredibly well for me.

Dave's report gives us an idea about how a BUDGET ACCOUNT can be used to save for a new car. A few of the main considerations to keep in mind are: 1. Even a very small monthly deposit—one you could actually laugh about—will get you mobilized in this endeavor; 2. Your monthly allocation can be increased whenever you believe you can afford to increase it (perhaps you can allocate a portion of an annual salary increase to this account); and 3. If you are so inclined, you may invest some or all of your "new car account" in some other financial asset, in the hope that dividends or a capital gain will speed you along toward your goal.

13. Clothing Account

Some people like to make frequent additions to their wardrobe, or replace items in their wardrobe with newer items. Sometimes people want to make a major wardrobe overhaul at a specific time, for instance at the start of a new job or the beginning of an academic year. People may want to make major wardrobe additions linked to an event, such as a graduation or wedding. Finally, some persons use clothing purchases as a way of nurturing themselves when they have encountered a major frustration or when they are low in spirits.

Whatever the reason, it is very clear that clothing is more than an occasional and minor expense with many people. In fact, in my many counseling experiences with persons for whom personal budgeting is an issue, clothing expenditure is one of the two most frequently occurring problem areas.

Let's hear from Kathy about her experiences as an example of some of the problems and possible solutions in this challenging area:

I just love clothes. I love everything about clothes. I like the way they look. I like the way they feel. I like seeing myself in something new. And, I love shopping for clothes. You may have heard the expression: "When the going gets tough, the tough go shopping." Well, that's me. At least, it **was** me. Things have changed...not entirely; but they've changed.

A few years ago I graduated and got a well-paying job. As a college student I had sometimes dressed up, but often I wore jeans and casual shirts. Well, when I became a professional, I figured I had to dress like a professional. You know..."dress for success."

At first it was under control. Once or twice a week I'd go shopping, and I'd only buy things that I knew I'd wear often and that were reasonably priced.

As time went on, I became less concerned about the price. After all, I had charge cards. And, I was sick and tired of passing by some stunning clothes just because they didn't go with things I already had. I'm embarrassed to say so, but I think I equated a stunning appearance with a good job performance. I secretly thought that if I could "knock 'em dead" with a great outfit every day, I'd advance professionally, and I'd earn enough to pay off all the charge card debts. I was spending about $600 a month for clothes.

It got even worse. When I felt blue, I'd go buy another pretty silk blouse to try to cheer myself up. You may think that this story ends up with my filing for bankruptcy. But no, just before it would have come to that, I came to my senses. It happened one night when I was about to send in an application for another charge card (I had charged three to the limit). I was looking over an account statement when I saw an identical charge posted three times in one week: $39.95 for a silk blouse. I got angry. "They're trying to cheat me!" Then I found them. The blouses, I mean. They were under a pile of other stuff, in three separate unopened bags. It hit me like a ton of bricks. I wasn't getting pleasure or satisfaction out of these clothes anymore. Buying them was just a habit.

I got some help. I thought I was going to have to spend a lot of time talking about my childhood and all. But we spent hardly any time on it. We took a practical approach: a BUDGET ACCOUNT. First, we used an amortization table and found out how much it was going to cost me per month to pay off my charge cards in 36 months. It came to $375 a month!

Next, we figured a reasonable amount per month for intermittent expenses like car repair, car insurance, holiday gifts, vacations, and membership dues. We also figured in an account for clothes, and allocated $30 a month for it (about one twentieth of what I *had been* spending).

I was putting aside $600 a month between my BUDGET ACCOUNT and my massive credit card payment. And I couldn't charge anything, because although I kept one credit card (I cut the others to ribbons), I promised myself it was only for emergencies or for something that I had money waiting for in my BUDGET ACCOUNT. Well, I started to fall behind financially right away, and to set things straight I had to share an apartment with a roommate and take my lunch to work most days. And that's the way things will be until I've paid off those charge cards.

I'm "living a little poorer" now, but I'm much happier. First of all, even though I'm under restraint as far as spending goes, I really feel a sense of control over my finances and my life. And secondly...you won't believe this! Even though I have only $360 per year to spend on clothes, I'm just loving shopping again! When I go in and buy something that I've been eyeing and saving for for three or four months, I get a tremendous sense of triumph! And I really value the few things I *can* buy. No more bags of silk blouses sitting around unopened! Every time I put on a piece of clothing I saved for methodically, I get a feeling of satisfaction. It's not the things I own that make me happy. It's the feeling of being in control of my finances and my life. The BUDGET ACCOUNT SYSTEM has turned my life around!

There's not much I can add to Kathy's story. But don't kid yourself into thinking that her story is unusual, or that many people don't end up in bankruptcy because of trying to make themselves okay by continually shopping for clothes or other items. They do. A monthly allocation into your BUDGET ACCOUNT for clothing will help you structure your spending. You may find yourself shopping more carefully, and therefore getting more clothing for your dollar. You may even end up valuing the clothes you *do* have much, much more.

14. The Hobby Account

Most people have at least one hobby of some kind or another. Hobbies can exist at any level of expense. If running is our hobby, the only significant expense (as long as we stay relatively injury-free) is a good pair of training shoes. If backpacking is our hobby, it may cost us several hundred dollars at first to outfit ourselves with a good backpack, tent, sleeping bag, hiking boots, and camping stove. And if our hobby is photography, stereo, or computers, we could easily spend up into the thousands.

A hobby can be a very meaningful part of a person's life. It can provide respite by allowing us to become deeply involved in some activity which has nothing to do with our work. It can fulfill a need which is left unmet by our work or family life. It can help us with our physical fitness, our finances, or the beauty or function of our home. In some cases it can even bring us a second income. It is extremely difficult to assign a value, in dollars, to a hobby. What we can do is to assign a value, in dollars, to what we can afford.

Rob had an interesting and challenging time coming to terms with the money he was spending on his hobby of woodworking. Let's let him tell us about it:

I love working with wood. I don't really like the persnickety finish work—the endless sanding and varnishing to give a piece a perfect finish. What I like is the creative part of a project. I like going into a room or a closet and thinking about what shape and size of cabinet, bookcase, or table would perfectly serve a purpose. Then I like figuring out how to put the piece together, and making diagrams of a sheet of plywood and figuring out how to cut out the pieces I need while leaving the smallest amount of waste. I like measuring, sawing, selecting fasteners...well, I guess you don't need to know all this. The point is I can really get absorbed into the creative process. It's a wonderful hobby for me. Since I earn a living sitting at a desk, it's a great change of pace.

It costs me a fair amount of money, all told, to support this hobby. Everything is fine now as far as the money is concerned. I have a BUDGET ACCOUNT, and I allocate $100 a month for my hobby: $70 for expendable goods like lumber, fasteners, and stain; and $30 for tools (especially power tools). Last year I allocated $80 a month for my hobby; next year I may go to $120. I really feel like I'm managing the situation intelligently now, and I'm completely comfortable with it. But a couple years ago it gave me fits.

I used to wait 'til the end of the month to see how much money I had left in my checking account when the next payday came around. Then, I'd spend it all on lumber, tools, etcetera. I thought I was using restraint and common sense, by waiting 'til payday.

Then expenses would come up, like vacations, holidays, and car repairs. I'd end up in the hole, and I'd use chargecards to buy tools and materials. Then I got the "brilliant idea" of building bookcases for sale. (That way I'd be doing what I loved, and earning the money to support the hobby as well!) It actually worked. . .for about two months. I was kind of excited about it. I felt like an entrepreneur. I began to dread getting home at night, because there it would be! All that **work**, waiting for me. Not an inviting pastime waiting for me. Not a creative challenge. Just work. I gave it up.

I began to be more aware of long term financial planning. I learned about the value of having whole or universal life insurance, an IRA, a tax sheltered annuity, and some other investments. I went into those instruments with gusto, but then I didn't have a dime to spend on lumber and other materials. I told myself that my financial future is more important, and that woodworking would have to wait. Boy, did I miss it!

Then I learned about the BUDGET ACCOUNT SYSTEM. Somehow, it helped me put things back into a balanced perspective. That's what I was missing: balance. I decided to set aside eighty dollars a month for my woodworking hobby, along with allotments for auto repair, vacations, etcetera. I had to reduce my contributions to my tax sheltered annuity, and to my other investments. But I know I'll gradually and intelligently build those up in time. My finances have balance now. They're balanced among day-to-day needs, my hobby, my financial future, and intermittent expenses. Now and then I sit down, look over my BUDGET ACCOUNT, and plan changes I may make in my finances. With the BUDGET ACCOUNT, it all feels so balanced. I feel so much in control of it. It's really satisfying and enjoyable. I can hardly express it.

Rob's story brings to mind an analogy. When water is in its liquid form, it's rather chaotic. If it is to freeze, the whole freezing process has to get started with six molecules arranging themselves into the hexagonal pattern that gives ice its structure. If one hexagon can't form, water won't freeze. If one forms, the rest can follow suit. One set of water molecules acts as the "prime mover." When a person begins a BUDGET ACCOUNT by managing one type of expense in the way prescribed by the system, it paves the way for the rest of the person's finances to fall into line just like the rest of the water molecules do when ice forms. In Rob's case, managing his hobby expenses via the BUDGET ACCOUNT was his prime mover.

15. Homeowner's Tax and Insurance Escrow Account

When most people buy a home, they take a note from a bank, savings and loan, or mortgage company.   They may be obliged, on a monthly basis along with their principle and interest payment, to put money into an escrow account. The lending institution maintains the escrow account for the homeowner, and pays the homeowner's property taxes and homeowner's insurance for him or her. (If the home buyer makes a "down payment" of at least 20 percent, then the lending institution does *not* require the escrow account. Home buyers can then assume responsibility for taxes and insurance themselves).

If you own your own home, and your lending institution does not require you to maintain a tax and insurance escrow account with them, you may want to maintain your own, using a BUDGET ACCOUNT. It could help you to avoid some discomfort when your taxes and your insurance premium are due.

16. Home Maintenance Account

If you own your own home, you probably have a homeowner's insurance policy. This would help you pay for repairs if a tree were to fall on your house, or if your house sustained damage in a severe storm, etcetera. But, what if your furnace were to wear out? What if your roof were to need replacement just because of years of wear and tear? What if your home has air conditioning, and the compressor were to wear out?

I'm not trying to ask you to think negatively, and I certainly don't want to be the bearer of ill tidings. But, if you own your home long enough, you will eventually encounter repair bills. You can, if you wish to, start setting aside some money each month in a BUDGET ACCOUNT for home repair. Even if you set aside a small amount and it does not entirely cover a repair bill, it will at least lessen the impact of the expense.

In this chapter I have described SIXTEEN possible uses for a BUDGET ACCOUNT. I am **not** suggesting that you set up a BUDGET ACCOUNT with all SIXTEEN categories. Remember, if you do have a regular income, you can probably absorb some of these expenses out of your regular monies. Or, in some cases you can use alternative financing. What I am suggesting is that you think about the different categories of expenses which can be managed through a BUDGET ACCOUNT, and that you choose the ones which you believe will help you the most. You may wish to make these choices according to your feelings. That is, use the BUDGET ACCOUNT for those types of intermittent expenses which make you feel the most uncomfortable when you are confronted with them.

Whichever types of expenses you choose to budget, I do hope you will give this system a good solid try. It has worked for me personally since I devised the system six years ago, and it has worked for many persons to whom I have taught it. Try it. You may find it to be very helpful and satisfying.

11 Managing Your Cash Flow "by Feel"

I have made the point a number of times that once you have allocated money to your BUDGET ACCOUNT for intermittent expenses, you will be able to "handle the rest of your budget by feel." Nora's story in Chapter 3 provides a hint about this process. And, in the section on "Managing Start-up Problems" in Chapter 9, Fred's story also illustrates the idea.

Do You Want to "Be a Bookkeeper"?

Without a BUDGET ACCOUNT to handle the intermittent stuff, our regular checking account balance is not very meaningful. If you were a business, and kept precise books, you would have lines for "cash on hand," "accounts payable," and "accounts receivable." The intermittent expenses which I am suggesting you handle through a BUDGET ACCOUNT are roughly the equivalent of a business' "accounts payable," and/or perhaps "encumbered funds." So, after subtracting your "accounts payable" and your "encumbered funds" from your cash on hand, you would derive a "bottom line," which would be a better indication of where you were financially at that moment in time.

How would you like to keep books on your own finances like that? With every passing month since your last automobile insurance payment you could regard one month's worth of insurance premium as either an "account payable" or an as "encumbered funds." It would take a lot of bookkeeping. And it doesn't sound like fun to me; it sounds like drudgery. But, without either that type of bookkeeping method or a BUDGET ACCOUNT, your check book balance lacks meaning.

"False Build-ups" and "Quick Drops"

For instance, you may find that as you approach the end of a month you have a couple hundred dollars more than usual. What does this mean? Does it mean you can afford to get those stereo speakers you've been wanting? Not necessarily. It could mean that your "cash on hand" has been building up because you haven't had to pay for any auto repairs recently (and one may be "lurking just around the bend"). Or, it could mean that your auto insurance payment is due next month, and not having to pay it for the past 5 months has increased your cash on hand.

> The greater the number and amounts of your intermittent expenses, the greater will be the variability of your regular checking account balance.

> You will have little notion as to what that balance really means about your month-to-month financial condition.

The BUDGET ACCOUNT can change all that :

For example, if you pay $600 per year for auto insurance and you're placing $50 per month into your BUDGET ACCOUNT for that purpose, then:

A. Neither are you experiencing a "false build-up" of $50 per month in your checking account;

B. Nor will you experience a "quick drop" of $300 in
your checking account balance when you pay the
premium.

If you spend an average of $2400 per year on travel and
vacations and are placing $200 per month into your
BUDGET ACCOUNT for that purpose, then:

A. Neither are you experiencing a "false build-up" of
$200 per month in your checking account;

B. Nor will you experience a "quick drop" in your
checking account balance due to being unprepared
for your next travel or vacation expense.

I hope that I have convinced you of the following:

1. Intermittent expenses will cause "false build-ups"
and "quick drops" in your cash flow, and will thus
make it very difficult, if not impossible, for you to
understand your month-to-month finances;

2. Once you have "filtered out the noise from the
signal" by setting aside funds for intermittent
expenses, what you have left in your cash flow
should be an understandable, meaningful figure;
and

3. By watching that understandable figure on a
month-to-month basis, you will easily see whether
you have either a) extra funds to save, invest, or
spend; or b) a shortfall requiring some reduction in
spending.

Confidence through the BUDGET ACCOUNT

If you have set up your BUDGET ACCOUNT to handle all significant intermittent expenses, and if your checking account balance decreases month to month, then you can have confidence in the conclusion that you are spending beyond your means somewhere, and need to cut some expenses.

Conversely, if your checking account balance increases month to month, you will know that your spending is within your means, and that you have some extra funds to save, invest, or spend.

Phil's experiences may be instructive:

> I've always been a pretty good wage earner, so in that way I've always done all right financially. But now that I keep my finances organized with a BUDGET ACCOUNT, I realize just how sloppy and haphazard I used to be with money. I'm mostly talking about the difference between wasting money and saving money.
>
> For me, the difference between wasting and saving is having a sense that savings are real. I know that may sound odd, but I'll bet many people experience the same thing. Let me try to explain it. Before I started the BUDGET ACCOUNT, I'd waste a lot of money because I didn't have any confidence that being more careful would make a difference. I'd be having a bite to eat with my friends, and I'd order a few beers, even though I didn't need them. Drinking beer in a restaurant is expensive! I knew that, but I'd say to myself,

"What's the difference? If I save it today I'll only have to spend it on a car repair or something tomorrow!" In other words, I didn't think the saving would be real.

Or, I'd have to buy some tires for my car. And I knew if I shopped around a bit, I could save fifteen or twenty dollars. But I'd say to myself, "What's the difference? If I save it today I'll only have to spend it tomorrow for a doctor's appointment or something!" Again, I just didn't have any sense that a saving could be real. I just felt that all my money was going to be sucked up by expenses one way or the other. So what was the use of trying to save some here or there? I know my thinking was totally senseless and illogical. But I'll bet a lot of other people do the same thing.

Well, now I've identified all the expenses that I used to think would come along unexpectedly and suck away any money I could save:

1. car repairs
2. doctor bills
3. vet bills
4. travel
5. holiday gifts
6. car insurance

So I started putting money away into a BUDGET ACCOUNT every month for those six kinds of expenses. Then I decided to try to keep my check book balance up to $400 at the end of every month. I knew that those six expenses couldn't come along and spoil my plans. Those expenses were already taken care of.

Well, first month I tried it my check book balance fell to $350. I just thought back on the month a bit. I didn't fool around with a lot of receipts and paperwork. I just thought about it. And I came to the conclusion that I was "throwing too much money out the window" in restaurants and bars. Well, I happen to like the feel of being in certain restaurants and bars. I didn't want to give it up, but I wanted my money managing to work out. So, I decided to try 3 things:

1. I estimated that I drank maybe 2 or 3 colas or ice teas per day in restaurants. At an average of 85 cents a crack, that's around $8.50 to $12.75 a week, or $34.00 to $51.00 a month! I figured to drink water, mostly.

2. I drink a few beers in restaurants and bars, sometimes 'cause I really want one, sometimes out of habit, or even because someone I'm with is having one. I figured I'd only order beer the times I *really* wanted one.

3. When I eat in a restaurant I always order just a little too much, 'cause I want the variety. You know, a sandwich'll be plenty, but I order fries with it. That kind of thing. So I figured to just order what I knew I needed, and to heck with the variety. Well, the next month my check book balance at the end of the month shot up

from $350 to $500! I never wrote things down or tallied them up or anything. But I estimate I saved $50 each on beer, soft drinks, and extra food (mostly fries). I took that extra $100 that was above the $400 I wanted to end the month with, and I put it into a new section of my BUDGET ACCOUNT that I called "For Something Special." And, that was just the first month!

Here's the thing. Before the BUDGET ACCOUNT, I just thought saving a buck here or there wouldn't make a difference. Now I know it makes a difference 'cause I've separated out the expenses that made it seem so hopeless, and I see the difference at the end of each month.

I kept it up, you know. I mean saving on beer, soft drinks, and extra food. In fact, I've made a kind of hobby out of finding little ways to save a buck here or there, because I *see* the difference, I *save* the difference, and most of all I've got *plans* for the difference. In fact, after 4 months I'd put $800 into that "for something special" account.

There was a lot for sale 15 miles outside of town: an acre and a half, right on the river. Fella that owned it said he bought it to build on, but that it was too wet. He couldn't get a permit for a year 'round home. He sold it to me for $600! I'm gonna fish and camp on it. On my own land! And who knows what it'll be worth in the future? It's amazing. I bought a piece of land with money I saved on beer and fries! And I

only saw the worth of saving it when the
BUDGET ACCOUNT put some sense into my
money.

In this chapter we've been learning how to "get a feel for our
budgets." We've discussed the way in which establishing a
BUDGET ACCOUNT protects our regular account from being
affected by the "false build-ups" and "quick drops" that
intermittent expenses would otherwise cause. And, we've
begun to discuss how we can build confidence in our analysis
of the money in our regular account. Having discussed the
rationale for a BUDGET ACCOUNT, having shown how to
set one up, and having illustrated its use, we've now essentially
turned our attention back to your regular checking account.

Phil's story illustrated quite a bit about this aspect of
budgeting. Let's hear from Kim, whose story may also be
helpful.

I'm a physical therapist, and I've been working in
my profession for about 5 years. When I first
started work, I got a modest apartment and, for the
first two years, I shared it with a roommate. I
bought a used car, and had it maintained regularly.
I was careful with my money, and after three years
I had about $12,000 in a savings account.

I knew I was doing okay, but I was real nervous
about money and about my financial future. So I
didn't even spend on things I felt I deserved. For
instance, I had a few travel opportunities. But I
passed them up. I had the money in my "savings
account," but I guess I didn't know what I was
"saving" for. I wanted so much to handle things in a

responsible way. I kept thinking things like "What if I need that money for retirement?" or "What if my car totally breaks down and I need to buy a new one?" or "What if there's a family emergency and I have to help out?" I kept passing up opportunities to spend for things that would have been fun or useful because I was so scared I'd be irresponsible. It was pretty weird. I was saving money that I was afraid to ever use.

If I hadn't learned about the BUDGET ACCOUNT SYSTEM, who knows? That savings account may have stayed there untouched (and useless to me) until I died. When I learned about the BUDGET ACCOUNT, I decided to set up my accounts as follows:

1.	Vacation	$ 80
2.	Emergency	$ 50
3.	New car	$ 50
4.	Auto insurance	$ 35
5.	Auto repair	$ 60
6.	Retirement	$100
7.	Dreams	$ 00
	T O T A L	$375

Now I know what my savings are for: they're for anything I want. I no longer worry about retirement; every year I'll take the $1200 I've put aside and deposit it into an Individual Retirement Account I've opened. I don't worry about family emergencies. I'm putting away $50 a month for that purpose, and it makes me feel responsible. I don't worry about a new car. I'm putting away $50 a month for one now, and I'll increase it next year. When I have a travel opportunity, I feel okay taking it, because I'm putting $80 a month aside for just that purpose.

You'll notice I have a "dreams account" in my BUDGET ACCOUNT, and you'll notice the number zero. I don't automatically put anything into it. Here's what I do. I've decided to keep a $500 minimum in my regular checking account. At the beginning of every month, I pay my bills and I make my BUDGET ACCOUNT transfer. Then I just go through my month, spending as I need to, keeping an eye on my balance. On the day I get my next paycheck, I look at my balance, and I write a check to myself for every penny over $500. So, if I have $610.50 in my regular checking account on payday, I write myself a check for $110.50. Then, I deposit it into my BUDGET ACCOUNT, and I credit my "dreams account."

Since I'm taking care of those other needs in my BUDGET ACCOUNT, this particular "dreams account" is for anything I want—more travel, investments, an eventual down payment on a home—who knows? But I know that it can be for whatever I think will fulfill my dreams. The other stuff is taken care of.

Another thing: by bringing my regular checking account balance down to exactly $500 at the end of every month, I start every month with the same amount. So, without even trying, I've figured out that I use an average of $15 per day for food and "incidentals." Incidentals include restaurants, magazine subscriptions, toiletries, gasoline for my car, birthday gifts, postage stamps...you know, everything that isn't a major bill or a BUDGET ACCOUNT item. So, by the 10th of the month, when I've paid my major bills and made by BUDGET ACCOUNT transfer, I need about $15 times 20 days equals $300 "walking around money" for the rest of the month. (I usually have more; I save almost every month.)

So, if it's the 22nd of a 30-day month, I know I'll probably need $120 (above the $500 minimum) to "walk around with." If I've got $700 left, then I figure "I'm $80 to the good." So if a friend asks me if I want to "spring for tickets to a concert," I can do it and I feel fine. I'm setting aside money for important responsibilities, so I can do what I want with the rest. That's what the BUDGET ACCOUNT has done for me: **I feel fine.**

Kim's story is a very good illustration of how we can end up "getting an accurate feel for our budgets" by using the BUDGET ACCOUNT. By taking off all the dollars over $500 at the end of the month, she starts every new month with the same amount.

First, she pays her major bills and makes her BUDGET ACCOUNT transfer. Then, as she puts it, "without even trying," she became aware of how much money she was using for food and "incidentals."

In Kim's case, when she ends the month with over $500, she transfers the amount over $500 to a "dreams account" within her BUDGET ACCOUNT. She says that her dreams account is for "anything I want—more travel, investments, an eventual down payment on a home—who knows?"

In Phil's case, reported earlier in this chapter, he kept a balance of $400 in his regular checking account. When payday arrived, he transferred the amount over $400 to his BUDGET ACCOUNT into a category he called "for something special." He eventually managed to buy a lot of land with his "for something special" account.

Both Phil's and Kim's stories have illustrated a number of points, including the following:

1. You can bring order and purpose to your personal budgeting by doing one thing: systematically setting aside funds for intermittent expenses (this is a key point in the BUDGET ACCOUNT SYSTEM).

2. By setting a minimum balance for yourself in your regular checking account, you can quickly learn whether you are underspending or overspending your available money. You can therefore easily manage your cash flow without extensive or detailed planning.

3. By transferring any dollars over your minimum balance at the beginning of a new month, you give yourself an opportunity to "budget by feel."

4. If you manage your cash flow in such a way as to end each month with dollars above your minimum balance, you can transfer the overage to an account of your choice.

5. The funds which you transfer to an account of your choice will feel like "unencumbered funds," since your BUDGET ACCOUNT is taking care of predictable needs. You can use these unencumbered funds in ways that are fulfilling to you, and this will give you even more incentive to trim expenses and save.

6. The BUDGET ACCOUNT SYSTEM can help you replace feelings of being frustrated, deprived, and defeated with feelings of control, mastery, and fulfillment. Study this book. Put the system to use in your life. Don't delay or miss out on the opportunity to manage your finances in ways which can be so fulfilling in both practical and psychological ways.

12 Marriage and the BUDGET ACCOUNT System

It is sometimes stated that all problems in marriages are attributable to sex, power, and money. I think the major issues of marriage are affection, respect, trust, good faith, appreciation, and shared values. But money matters are clearly relevant to those issues. No attempt will be made here to discount or trivialize the intense and complicated issues which can occur in marriages. I am **not** going to imply that if a couple can take away their tensions and arguments about money that all will be well. What I **will** say is that if a couple can agree on their use of money, then at least money can be removed as an issue, and they can concentrate on the more fundamentally important ones.

One of the Fundamental Realities of Marriage

On the face of it, it seems almost unnecessary to describe some of the themes of money difficulties experienced by couples. They are thought of as "common knowledge." They are often the subject of situation comedies and also of stand-up comics. However, although making light of the topic may relieve tension about it in the short term, it may also trivialize the issue and make it more difficult to discuss and negotiate in the long term. Finances are one of the fundamental realities of marriage: we live together and share expenses. We live in a world in which almost everything we eat, drink, drive, live in, and play with is available only via the accepted medium of exchange. We may pool our monies into common bank accounts, and every expenditure one person makes reduces their partner's available resources.

Marriage and Money: Some Practical Considerations

Here are four types of money situations which can occur in a marriage:

A. One partner supports the other, and therefore provides all the funds for common expenses and discretionary money.

B. The partners earn the same amount of money. They therefore contribute equally to common expenses and have the same amount of discretionary money.

C. One partner earns more than the other. The partners each contribute the same amount to common expenses. The higher earning partner has more discretionary money.

D. One partner earns more than the other. The partners each keep the same amount of discretionary money. The higher earning partner contributes more to common expenses.

It is beyond the scope of this book to comment on the relative merits of each of the four above-described situations. That treatment of the material would be the subject of a book specifically on relationships, not of a book specifically on budgeting. I **will** make the following two comments:

1. Potential marriage partners are well advised to talk about these possible financial arrangements. Their beliefs and feelings about these matters will surface inevitably, and would best be discussed before the marriage commitment is made. An initial lack of agreement is not necessarily a problem. Expressing their feelings and hearing their partner's feelings may help turn an initial disagreement into a workable understanding.

2. There are many potential ways in which two persons can meet one another's romantic and partnership needs. Financial equality prior to marriage is not a necessity for a "good match."

Marriage without the BUDGET ACCOUNT SYSTEM

Marriage can serve as an amplifier. The common future, the interdependence, and even the very proximity of married life all typically lead to an intensification of feelings and issues. The more issues which can be made into non-issues, the better off the partners are. But if money issues are unresolved, they can threaten the good will and respect in the relationship.

If we have placed some or all of our financial resources into one common place for disbursement, then there is potential for questioning one another and even resenting one another's decisions. Here are just a few of the common complaints expressed by married persons:

a. When I work so hard to earn a living, I resent seeing my partner order extravagantly in a restaurant.

b. I resent my partner telling me to try to repair an old item rather than just letting me buy a new one.

c. I resent seeing my partner spending so much on current conveniences when I had hoped we'd be saving for something really important in the future.

d. We've been cooperating to save money. But now it's time to spend some on a great vacation and my partner insists that the savings are for our retirement.

e. We both want to save for a down payment on a home. But my partner does not seem to be willing to control spending in the present to save more, while I am.

f. We each spend on things for ourselves, and we don't "keep track." But sometimes I feel that my partner wastes more money than I do.

These types of perceptions and feelings can lead to a disruption of the good faith and respect in a marriage. They can, and often do, lead to arguments and accusations. A specific expenditure regarded by one's partner as extravagant may not in itself be a major issue. However, if the perceived extravagance is seen as a disregard or disrespect of one's efforts, wishes, or feelings, then it can touch off a major issue.

Without either 1) an extremely flexible attitude about money on the part of both partners, or 2) a workable agreement regarding expenditures, money issues are a likely source of relationship problems.

Marriage with a BUDGET ACCOUNT SYSTEM

Here are a few examples of the ways in which a BUDGET ACCOUNT can be put to productive use in a marital relationship:

1. If partners agree on a particular goal or dream, they can make a monthly contribution to an account held aside specifically for that purpose. This practice can prevent the situation in which one person assumes their partner is as serious as they about saving for a dream, only to experience disappointment and frustration when the partner uses funds for other purposes.

Bill and Laura experienced such an issue. Laura's story about it illustrates the point:

> From the first time we talked about being married, Bill and I agreed on a mutual goal of someday having a vacation home in the mountains. We both felt that modern-day life is hectic and industrialized. We both felt that to someday have a mountain hideaway would be a wonderful thing for our lifestyle. And I thought we had pretty much agreed that it was a high priority—and that we would save our money for it.
>
> Well, we were both working. I was handling the checking account register, but we both carried checks. I was really excited because with both of us working, we had more than enough money for our needs, and we could begin putting money into a savings account for our dream house in the mountains.

We saved about two hundred a month for two months. Then, I began to bring my lunch to work and to economize in other ways, because I was excited about the progress we were making at saving. Then, it happened. First, right near the end of the month when I was looking at how much we could save, Bill came home with a new and expensive softball glove. I mean a really expensive one. It really cut away a lot of what we could save that month. I asked him about it and he just said "It will really improve my game." So, I hid my disappointment and forgot it.

Well, next month I kept up my economy measures to maximize savings. And again, just as I was calculating how much we could save, Bill made a pretty big purchase. This time it was lamb skin seat covers for his car. They were nice looking, but I just didn't see the value of them, especially compared with the value that I thought we'd agreed we'd get someday from buying a mountain retreat home. I asked Bill about it, and he got angry and said "Hey, I earn money and I can spend some if I like." I was starting to really resent things. First of all, we had agreed that we were going to save for a dream. Second, I was denying myself certain luxuries and conveniences to maximize savings. And third, here's Bill spending on luxuries while I'm scrimping to save. I was angry, but I just dropped it.

Well, it happened again. This time, it wasn't one $100 check for a purchase. It was four $20 checks for cash. I asked Bill what the $80 was for, and he said "Beer and pizza after softball games." I said that it seemed extravagant when I was making my own lunches and taking other economy measures to help us save for our mountain home. Bill got angry. He said there would always be plenty of time to save for a mountain home, and he accused me of being "controlling" and of being a drag. Well, I hit the roof! I accused him of being irresponsible and of changing our plans without even consulting me.

The argument got pretty hostile. We both felt that we had been treated unfairly by the other. After things finally got cooled down, Bill explained to me that he had never felt carefree about leisure time or about spending money on himself, and that playing softball and having pizza and beer after the games felt like a very important freedom for him. He admitted that "the lamb skin seat covers were unnecessary and stupid."

I explained that I have always dreamed of a vacation home, that I thought we had agreed on its importance. I told Bill that I felt "put upon" and taken for granted when he spent money freely while I was economizing. He understood my feelings and I understood his. We tried making some agreements about spending. They didn't work out too well, though. First of all, they were so hard to monitor. And secondly, intermittent expenses came along (we hadn't planned on them, and we argued about how to handle them). But things worked out fine once we learned the BUDGET ACCOUNT SYSTEM.

Here's what we do now. We still use the same
regular checking account, but we have a BUDGET
ACCOUNT as well. Within the BUDGET
ACCOUNT we have a "vacation home account,"
and we put $225 into it every month. (We'll
increase it to $250 or $275 after we've gotten pay
raises). Then, we pay our major bills, make a few
other BUDGET ACCOUNT allocations (car repair,
car insurance, gifts, and vacation), and estimate
other household expenses. Whatever is left we
divide up between us as spending money. We've
agreed that we will **not** question one another on
how this money is spent. If I want to economize
and add some of my spending money to the
vacation home account, that's my business. But I
can't demand that Bill do the same. And if Bill
wants to spend on things that I might consider
extravagant, it's none of my business as long as he
stays within his spending money.

We have no more conflicts over money. We
understand one another's feelings on the matter,
and we've set up a system which meets both our
needs. Bill sometimes wishes he had a little more
"mad money," but he admits that the vacation
home account will be a major advantage someday.
I sometimes wish we were saving a little faster, but I
admit that Bill's feeling freer about leisure spending
is important for his overall feelings about his life.
The best thing of all is that there's a sense of good
will and respect between us again. It's amazing that
a simple thing like a BUDGET ACCOUNT can
help clear away money issues and set the stage for
a resumption of good feelings in a marriage.

2. Sometimes marriage partners value different things—
   that is, material things which can be purchased. If they
   understand their own preferences but not their
   partner's, this can lead to a loss of respect. And, if
   they feel that their resources are being squandered by
   their partners' material preferences, then resentment
   and conflict can ensue.

Roger and Jean experienced this issue. Roger's story about it
illustrates this point:

> Jean and I had been married about a year or so
> when it became apparent to me that things weren't
> okay as far as money was concerned. Jean and I
> both work, and we pool our money and work out
> of a joint checking account. All of our bills are paid
> with joint money, and that's fine. But, our
> individual expenses had become a problem.
>
> Jean is concerned about her appearance, and she
> spends for things like "perms" for her hair and
> clothing. Lots of clothing. I think she has great
> taste in clothes; everything she picks out is
> attractive. She boasts that she always buys things
> "on sale" and "never pays full price."
>
> Jean spends considerable time and money on
> clothes. The time is something I don't resent. She
> really seems to enjoy it; it's a form of entertainment
> for her, and it's not up to me to tell Jean what to
> choose for a pastime. It's the total amount of
> money she spends that I resent. I'm sure she
> spends what most reasonable people would call an
> unreasonable amount for a couple with our income.

Problems would ensue. For example, we would be hit with an unexpected car repair, and we wouldn't have enough of a checking account balance to cover it. Or, we'd have travel expenses, holiday gift expenses, or an auto insurance premium due, and we wouldn't have the balance to cover it. So, we would end up using credit cards, and we would struggle, and fight with each other, while trying to pay them off. I felt that our lack of sufficient checking account balances to pay these expenses was due to her excessive clothing purchases. She disagreed.

When I try to talk with Jean about this issue she gets pretty defensive. She counters my concerns with two types of arguments:

1) She insists that the clothes she buys are "an investment and a good value." She says they're an investment because the better she dresses, the better she'll do in her profession. She likes the expression "dress for success."

2) She insists that she doesn't spend any more on clothing than I spend on my boat and fishing equipment.

At first, I tried to discuss the matter with her on logical grounds. For instance, I pointed out that a decent boat and trailer can always be re-sold for a substantial portion of their original cost, whereas clothing, even if purchased at "bargain basement prices," can never be re-sold at anything close to their cost. She was unmoved by this argument.

I also argued that while my boat purchase had been expensive, the continuing equipment purchases were quite modest. Compared to her clothing purchases, I only bought what I needed to pursue my hobby. She, on the other hand, purchased far more outfits than she needed to "dress for success." She was unmoved by this argument as well.

Now, before you get the wrong impression, I love Jean and see in her many charming and admirable qualities. Even though her behavior regarding clothing and money frustrated me, it wasn't the entire picture of our marriage. But the money problem had to be resolved, and I was never going to get her to change through discussion alone.

When I attended a seminar on the BUDGET ACCOUNT SYSTEM, I was sure I had the answer. I convinced Jean to give it a try. Now we have a BUDGET ACCOUNT. Within it, we have seven accounts, as follows:

1.	Auto repair	75/month
2.	Auto Insurance	65/month
3.	Vacation	90/month
4.	Holiday gifts	40/month
5.	New car escrow	50/month
6.	Jean's clothes	90/month
7.	Roger's boat & fishing	90/month
	T O T A L	$500/month

Every month, we have $500 placed into our BUDGET ACCOUNT. We credit it to the 7 accounts as shown above. We use our regular account for our typical bills, food, entertainment, and pocket money. We use the BUDGET ACCOUNT exclusively for the purposes listed. We have agreed that I am not to spend more for boating and fishing than the money allotted in "Roger's boat and fishing account," and that she is not to spend more on clothing than the money allotted in "Jean's clothing account."

We've had no difficulties with the types of expenses that we're now budgeting for. When an expense comes up, one of us writes the check and debits the appropriate account. There's absolutely no conflict between us anymore just because of an auto repair or any of those expenses covered by the BUDGET ACCOUNT.

Jean had to cut back her spending a bit, and she groused about it for awhile, but she knows it's fair. My boating and fishing account is building up quite a balance, which is my money to use as I please. Jean sees this, and I suspect that she now realizes that I was right about our comparative spending. But, I won't ask her to admit it. After all, **the purpose of the BUDGET ACCOUNT SYSTEM in a marriage is not to win or to be right**. The purpose is to take away money issues as a source of conflict, and it's working wonders for us.

These two stories should serve to illustrate some of the ways in which the BUDGET ACCOUNT SYSTEM has helped married couples to neutralize financial issues in their relationships. Of course, all the examples of BUDGET ACCOUNT uses shared in this volume are relevant to married life as well as single life.

13 Questions and Answers

So, if I open a BUDGET ACCOUNT, I'll have two check books?

That's correct. You'll have your "regular check book," and your BUDGET ACCOUNT check book. From your regular check book, you'll write a normal number of checks, perhaps between twenty and forty per month. From your BUDGET ACCOUNT check book, you'll write **far fewer** checks. It will of course depend on the use which you make of the BUDGET ACCOUNT, but two to five checks per month would be typical.

In Chapter 5, you first said to put money into coffee cans. Then, you said you were kidding. What if I really wanted to use coffee cans? Would that be okay?

Of course it would be okay. You could label the coffee cans, and put your monthly allocation into them each month in actual cash. Then, I guess the most convenient way to go about it would be to write out a check for a budgeted expense, for instance an auto repair. Then you would take the cash out of your "auto repair coffee can" and deposit it into your checking account to reimburse yourself. For holiday gifts, you could take the actual cash out of the "holiday gift coffee can" and take that cash shopping with you.

Even though I was only using the coffee can idea as an illustration, you could actually do it that way, though I don't highly recommend it. Here are a few disadvantages:

A. Cash is more subject to loss or theft than are deposits in a checking account.

B. You would lose out on the interest which you should be able to get in a checking account. (Most banks and savings and loans will pay interest on checking accounts with a high enough average daily balance. Because of its nature, your BUDGET ACCOUNT is likely to qualify for interest).

C. Once you get the hang of it, the minimal bookkeeping needed to manage a BUDGET ACCOUNT will be easy. And, it will be easier to leaf through the pages of your looseleaf notebook to see your account balances than it would be to count the cash in your coffee cans.

However, even though I recommend a BUDGET ACCOUNT checking account over the use of coffee cans, you could still use the cans. What are most important are the feelings of control, mastery, and self-esteem which you will have when you have put the system into operation.

As I understand it, if I set up a BUDGET ACCOUNT to handle, say, five different types of expenses, I will end up keeping track of those five separate accounts by using five recording sheets like those you used as illustrations in Chapter 6. And that's it? Five recording sheets?

That's right. One recording sheet for each account. Of course, when a sheet gets full, you'll start a fresh one, but only 5 sheets will be in use at a time. You may want to keep the used ones to look back at to analyze how things are working.

Having another check book means another checking account to balance each month. I can handle that. But won't I also have to reconcile the BUDGET ACCOUNT check book with the total of those recording sheets? What problems might I encounter?

Yes, you will have to reconcile the two. First of all, your BUDGET ACCOUNT check book, though very important, is typically not very active, so balancing it should usually be easy. Then, just get out a piece of scrap paper, go through your BUDGET ACCOUNT looseleaf, and jot down the current balances. Add them up and compare them to your current check book balance.

During your first few months, you may have discrepancies. Here are a few to look for:

A. Interest. You may have to remind yourself to credit one of your accounts with the monthly interest.

B. Forgetting to debit an account for a check written. You are not used to first writing a check and then recording the amount of that check in a place other than your check book register. You may forget at first. When there's a discrepancy, go through your check book register to see the checks you've written, and then be sure you've debited one of your recording sheets for the expense.

C. Forgetting to credit your accounts or your check register with your monthly allocation. Remember, the recommended procedure is to have an amount of money transferred from your "regular checking account" to your

BUDGET ACCOUNT each month. You'll have to make a habit of 1) debiting your regular check book, 2) crediting your BUDGET ACCOUNT check book, and 3) crediting your account recording sheets with their monthly allocations. It will take 2 to 5 minutes. It's just a matter of learning to do it regularly.

Once you have had the BUDGET ACCOUNT SYSTEM in operation for a few months, the minimal bookkeeping that it entails will become second nature to you. And, there is far less bookkeeping than you would experience with any other personal budgeting method that I have ever been aware of.

I am intrigued with the use of a BUDGET ACCOUNT to manage car expenses. Specifically, I'm interested in how the BUDGET ACCOUNT can help me make the decision of whether to keep putting money into a used car or buy a new one.

This is an excellent question, and it opens up an issue which could lead to considerable savings for you. As a psychologist, I can tell you that we human beings tend to believe in and live by our casual observations and our impressions. In some ways we are capable of accurate observations while in others we tend to be phenomenally inaccurate. Perhaps it is the emotional attachment which so many persons have to the idea of a new car, but people tend to overestimate the amount of money they spend maintaining a used car compared to the amount needed to purchase a new one.

I think Pete's story will shed some light on this for you:

> I began by BUDGET ACCOUNT in January of 1988, and I started out putting $50 per month into my auto repair account. I have a 1982 Dodge

Charger which was almost 6 years old when I began my BUDGET ACCOUNT. Everything was going fine until September of '89, when I had to have the engine overhauled. I wondered then whether I should get the work done or get a new car, and I talked it over with my mechanic. I decided to keep the used car running.

The engine overhaul cost me $900, which was a lot more than I had in my "auto repair account." Well, I paid the bill by BUDGET ACCOUNT check, and my auto repair account was running a deficit. I paid an extra $300 into my BUDGET ACCOUNT, and I increased my monthly allocation to $75. I caught up and got my auto repair account "into the black" again, and cut my monthly allocation to auto repair back to $60.

Then, just last October I ran into another major repair. My auto repair balance couldn't cover it, and I ran a deficit again. I covered it with an extra allocation again, this one for $200. I'm dead certain that if I weren't using a BUDGET ACCOUNT, I would have concluded that I'd been "throwing good money after bad," and that I'd been spending more money keeping this car up than it would have cost me to buy a new one. I'm sure that I would have figured it out that way subjectively. And, guess what? Since all the deposits and expenditures are right there on the recording sheets in my notebook, I added it up to see. Even with the two major repairs and extra allocations, and even with the $75 a month I put in for nine months, I've spent $3325 on maintenance

on that car over 40 months. That comes to $83
per month. That's a lot for maintenance, but have
you seen any new cars for $83 per month? Add to
that the fact that my auto insurance is low, as is the
property tax I pay when I register my car, and I'm
saving big money.

Subjectively you may be sure you're spending too much
maintaining a used car, but with a BUDGET ACCOUNT to
help you manage those expenses and keep track, you may
find that your impressions are inaccurate and you're doing
great keeping your used car maintained and running.

**Why should I bother to budget my money so as to
have enough for certain expenses ? Why is money
important, anyway ?**

It isn't. But privilege is. And money bestows privilege. Here
are a few of the privileges which money can bestow:

1. Vista. That is, a home with a view. I have often argued that
    an expensive and ostentatious house won't make anyone
    happy. But, a home with a view, particularly a view of a
    mountain or a body of water, may have a genuine and
    positive effect on a person's happiness and quality of life!
    Home sites with a view are typically more expensive.

2. Access to quality medical care. Most working and retired
    Americans have access to medical care; but there are
    occasions when difficult medical problems may result in
    our wanting to find the best medical care available. This
    may entail travel, or payment for services not covered by
    our medical insurance. Thus, access to quality medical
    care may at times be a privilege to which we are entitled
    only if we have access to the funds to pay for it.

3. Leisure time. Many of us have to work more than a typical 40-hour week, and may even have to limit vacation time. The opportunity for leisure time, or the ability to be sufficiently worry-free to enjoy it, are more available if we have sufficient money.

I like the idea of using a BUDGET ACCOUNT to save for a big dream like a vacation home. But how do I know how much money I'll accumulate, with interest, over a period of years ?

Use a compound interest table. For your convenience, I have included two of them in Appendices 5 and 6 on pages 103 and 104. The table in Appendix 5 shows the amount to which one dollar will accumulate, given the number of years and the interest rate you select. The table in Appendix 6 shows the amount to which one dollar, **deposited at the beginning of each year**, will accumulate.

These tables will be a very valuable aid in your evaluating a number of financial and economic situations. Let's take your example: saving for a vacation home. As an illustration, let's say that you will be saving $100 per month, and that you want to know how much money you will have after 15 years, with a predicted interest rate of 7%. First of all, the table in Appendix 6 helps you calculate the amount to which a dollar, deposited at the beginning of each year, will accumulate. So, let's be conservative and calculate $1200 per year for 14 years. Look at Appendix 6, and find the factor for 14 years and 7%. The factor is 24.13. So, we multiply $1200 times 24.13, and we get $28,956. This is the amount you can expect to accumulate.

Let's show how you can use both tables to make a calculation. Once again, suppose you want to save $100 per month for 15 years. But, this time let's say that your Uncle Al has given you a gift of $5000, and that you want to save that money as well. We already know that your own $1200 per year will build to $28,956 at 7%. Now, look up the factor for 15 years at 7% in the table in Appendix 5. It's 2.76. So, 2.76 times $5000 is $13,800.

Your uncle's gift to you builds to	$13,800
Your own savings build to	<u>$28,956</u>
T O T A L	$42,756

You can utilize these compound interest tables in a number of ways to make calculations about savings, to evaluate insurance policies or annuities, or to calculate what an asset such as a home would be worth given a certain rate of appreciation. (Don't forget to factor income tax on interest into your plans). This little resource may help you immeasurably in making your own financial plans.

Author's Concluding Comment

It is my hope that you will put the BUDGET ACCOUNT SYSTEM into use. It has great potential, not only for money management per se, but for giving you a sense of mastery and control over one of life's important tasks. And that has great potential for helping your self-esteem. Do the best you can to put aside any self-criticisms for your money management to date, and give yourself a fresh start with this method. You'll be very glad you did. Good luck!

Appendix 1

$50/month as of 4/86
___/month as of ___

AUTO REPAIR
NAME OF ACCOUNT

Date	Transaction	Credits	Debits	Balance
4/10/86	Initial Deposit	$150.00		$150.00
5/10/86	Auto. Dep.	$50.00		$200.00
5/24/86	check #101 to Athens Auto			
	Air for evaporator & drier		$102.78	$97.22
6/10/86	Auto. Dep.	$50.00		$147.22
6/14/86	Check #105 to Ace's Garage			
	for lube, tune-up		$59.15	$88.07
7/10/86	Auto. Dep.	$50.00		$138.07
8/10/86	Auto. Dep.	$50.00		$188.07
8/29/86	check #112 to Sears			
	for Diehard Battery		$59.95	$128.12
8/31/86	check #114 to Athens			
	Bandag for 2 new tires		$82.50	$45.62
9/10/86	Auto. Dep.	$50.00		$95.62
9/19/86	check #116 to Ace's			
	Garage to repair radiator			
	leak & replace radiator cap		$24.50	$71.12

Appendix 2

$75/month as of 4/86
___/month as of ___

V A C A T I O N
NAME OF ACCOUNT

DATE	TRANSACTION	CREDITS	DEBITS	BALANCE
4/10/86	Initital Deposit	$225.00		$225.00
5/10/86	Auto Deposit	$75.00		$300.00
6/10/86	Auto Deposit	$75.00		$375.00
7/10/86	Auto Deposit	$75.00		$450.00
7/15/86	Check #110 to W.W. Travel			
	for Plane Fare		$159.00	$291.00
7/19/86	Check #111 to Fulton Federal			
	for Traveler Checks		$200.00	$91.00
8/10/86	Auto Deposit	$75.00		$166.00
9/10/86	Auto Deposit	$75.00		$241.00
9/16/86	Check #115 to VISA to pay			
	for charged vacation			
	EXPENSES		$150.00	$91.00
10/10/86	Auto Deposit	$75.00		$166.00
11/10/86	Auto Deposit	$75.00		$241.00
12/10/86	Auto Deposit	$75.00		$316.00

Appendix 3

Temporary Account for Handling
1986 Tax Return
NAME OF ACCOUNT

Date	Transaction	Credits	Debits	Balance
5/29/87	Rec'd federal tax refund	$652.00		$652.00
8/3/87	check #241 to W.W.Travel			
	for vacation air fare		$386.00	$266.00
9/22/87	check #249 for cash			
	for purchase of collectibles		$100.00	$166.00
11/20/87	check #265 to VISA to			
	pay off charge for			
	Stereo Speakers		$166.00	$0.00

Appendix 4

BUDGET ACCOUNT WORKSHEET

Type of Occasional Expense or Name of Account	monthly amount	monthly amount	monthly amount	monthly amount	monthly amount
T O T A L					

APPENDIX 5

COMPOUND INTEREST TABLE

Amount to which $1.00 Will Accumulate at the End
of the Number of Years Shown

YEARS	4%	5%	6%	7%	8%	9%	10%
1	1.04	1.05	1.06	1.07	1.08	1.09	1.10
2	1.08	1.10	1.12	1.15	1.17	1.19	1.21
3	1.13	1.15	1.19	1.23	1.26	1.30	1.33
4	1.17	1.22	1.26	1.31	1.36	1.41	1.47
5	1.22	1.28	1.34	1.40	1.47	1.54	1.61
6	1.27	1.34	1.42	1.50	1.59	1.68	1.77
7	1.32	1.41	1.50	1.61	1.71	1.83	1.95
8	1.37	1.48	1.59	1.72	1.85	1.99	2.14
9	1.42	1.55	1.69	1.84	2.00	2.17	2.36
10	1.48	1.63	1.79	1.97	2.16	2.37	2.59
11	1.54	1.71	1.90	2.11	2.33	2.58	2.85
12	1.60	1.80	2.01	2.25	2.52	2.81	3.14
13	1.67	1.89	2.13	2.41	2.72	3.07	3.45
14	1.73	1.98	2.26	2.58	2.94	3.34	3.80
15	1.80	2.08	2.40	2.76	3.17	3.64	4.18
16	1.87	2.18	2.54	2.95	3.43	3.97	4.60
17	1.95	2.29	2.69	3.16	3.70	4.33	5.05
18	2.03	2.41	2.85	3.38	4.00	4.72	5.56
19	2.11	2.53	3.03	3.62	4.32	5.14	6.12
20	2.19	2.65	3.21	3.87	4.66	5.60	6.73
21	2.28	2.79	3.40	4.14	5.03	6.11	7.40
22	2.37	2.93	3.60	4.43	5.44	6.66	8.14
23	2.47	3.07	3.82	4.74	5.87	7.26	8.95
24	2.56	3.23	4.05	5.07	6.34	7.91	9.85
25	2.67	3.39	4.29	5.43	6.85	8.62	10.84
26	2.77	3.56	4.55	5.81	7.40	9.40	11.92
27	2.88	3.73	4.82	6.21	7.94	10.25	13.11
28	3.00	3.92	5.11	6.65	8.63	11.17	14.42
29	3.12	4.12	5.42	7.11	9.32	12.17	15.86
30	3.24	4.32	5.74	7.61	10.06	13.27	17.45

APPENDIX 6

COMPOUND INTEREST TABLE

Amount to which $1.00 Deposited at the Beginning of Each Year
Will Accumulate to at the End of the Number of Years Shown

YEARS	4%	5%	6%	7%	8%	9%	10%
1	1.04	1.05	1.06	1.07	1.08	1.09	1.10
2	2.12	2.13	2.18	2.22	2.25	2.28	2.31
3	3.25	3.31	3.38	3.44	3.51	3.57	3.64
4	4.42	4.53	4.64	4.75	4.87	4.99	5.11
5	5.63	5.80	5.98	6.15	6.34	6.52	6.72
6	6.90	7.14	7.39	7.65	7.92	8.20	8.49
7	8.21	8.55	8.90	9.26	9.64	10.03	10.44
8	9.58	10.03	10.49	10.98	11.49	12.02	12.58
9	11.00	11.58	12.18	12.82	13.49	14.19	14.94
10	12.49	13.21	13.97	14.78	15.65	16.56	17.53
11	14.03	14.92	15.87	16.89	17.98	19.14	20.38
12	15.63	16.71	17.88	19.14	20.50	21.95	23.52
13	17.29	18.60	20.02	21.55	23.22	25.02	26.98
14	19.02	20.58	22.28	24.13	26.15	28.36	30.77
15	20.83	22.66	24.67	26.89	29.32	32.00	34.95
16	22.70	24.84	27.21	29.84	32.75	35.97	39.55
17	24.65	27.13	29.91	33.00	36.45	40.30	44.60
18	26.67	29.54	32.76	36.38	40.45	45.02	50.16
19	28.78	32.07	35.79	40.00	44.76	50.16	56.28
20	30.97	34.72	38.99	43.87	49.42	55.77	63.00
21	33.25	37.51	42.39	48.01	54.46	61.87	70.49
22	35.51	40.40	45.99	52.47	58.90	66.56	78.54
23	38.08	43.50	49.82	57.18	65.77	75.79	87.50
24	40.65	46.73	53.87	62.25	72.11	83.70	97.35
25	43.31	50.11	58.16	67.68	78.95	92.32	108.18
26	46.08	53.67	62.71	73.48	86.35	101.72	120.10
27	48.97	57.40	67.52	79.70	94.34	111.97	133.21
28	51.97	61.32	72.64	86.35	102.97	123.14	147.63
29	55.04	65.44	78.06	93.46	112.23	135.30	163.49
30	58.33	69.76	83.80	101.07	122.35	148.58	180.94

More Quality Books from R & E Publishers

CURE YOUR MONEY ILLS: Improve Your Self-Esteem Through Personal Budgeting by Michael R. Slavit, Ph.D. Money is not the root of all evil, but the mishandling of it is a leading cause of emotional upheaval and marital breakups.This insightful work can help you to get control of your money and your life. Written by a psychologist who has taught money management techniques at the college level and in professional seminars, this book will help you to understand why you spend money the way you do and show you how to use it to meet your daily expenses, put aside money for vacations, save for a rainy day and be prepared for the occasional surprise monsoon.

$7.95	LC 91-50987	ISBN 0-88247-915-6
Trade Paper	6x9	Order #915-6

HOW TO BUY AND SELL REAL ESTATE: A Do-It-Yourself Survival Guide by Dorothy Carrel Qualls. You don't need a real estate agent to make profitable decisions. In fact, relying on an agent's advice can be disastrous.

Ms. Qualls is a broker who has bought and sold property throughout the country. Her book will help you avoid costly pitfalls while putting money in your pocket. Whether you are buying or selling a home, or investing in property, this book will guide you through every step of the process, from locating a property to signing the final papers.

$12.95	LC 91-50693	ISBN 0-88247-895-8
Trade Paper	6 x 9	Order #895-8

EASY MONEY: Reagan's Roaring 80's and the Overbuilding of America by D. Patrick Gallagher. The disastrous economic policies of the Reagan era that precipitated the collapse of the S&L's now threatens to destroy the commercial banks, the FDIC and insurance companies.

Deregulation of the financial industry created a feeding frenzy of banks and insurance companies who made reckless loans to commercial developers in order to make huge upfront fees. This situation was exacerbated when real estate developers were allowed to own S&L's. As a result, commercial property was overbuilt, causing the collapse of the commercial real estate market, leaving banks, insurance companies and you, holding the financial bag.

$14.95	LC 91-50685	ISBN 0-88247-903-4
Trade Paper	6 x 9	Order #903-4

WHAT WORKS: 5 Steps to Personal Power by William A. Courtney. Life is simple—if you know *What Works* and what doesn't.

This power packed action guide is a handbook for creating your dreams. Based on time tested universal principles, this book will guide you through the five steps of personal power. Once you master these simple principles, you will be able to create anything you want, from better health, to financial success, to deeper, more loving relationships.

$7.95	LC 91-50983	ISBN 0-88247-910-5
Trade Paper	6 x 9	Order #910-5

THE GOAL BOOK: Your Simple Power Guide to Reach any Goal & Get What You Want by James Hall. Would you like to be able to turn your dreams into realities? You can if you have concrete goals. This book is based upon a unique goal achievement technique developed by a high school teacher and career counselor in California's Silicon Valley. "Action Conditioning Technology" (ACT) will help you convert your dreams and wishful fantasies into obtainable goals. With this new achievement technology, you will be able to decide exactly what you want, what steps you need to take and when you will reach your objective.

$6.95	LC 91-50675	ISBN 0-88247-892-3
Trade paper	6 x 9	Order #892-3